the CENTER for

heRmeneutical studies

in H E L L E N I S T I C and M O D E R N C U L T U R E

The GRADUATE THEOLOGICAL UNION & The UNIVERSITY of CALIFORNIA

BERKELEY, CALIFORNIA

PROTOCOL OF THE THIRTY-SIXTH COLLOQUY: 3 JUNE 1979

S O U L   A N D   B O D Y   I N   S T O I C I S M

A. A. LONG

GLADSTONE PROFESSOR OF GREEK, UNIVERSITY OF LIVERPOOL, ENGLAND
VISITING MEMBER, INSTITUTE FOR ADVANCED STUDY, PRINCETON, N.J.

EDWARD C. HOBBS & WILHELM WUELLNER, *Editors*

McCORMICK THEOLOGICAL SEMINARY
1100 EAST 55th STREET
CHICAGO, ILLINOIS 60615

Copyright Ⓒ 1980 by CENTER FOR HERMENEUTICAL STUDIES

All rights reserved

ISSN   0098-0900

Key title:

Protocol of the colloquy of the Center for Hermeneutical Studies
in Hellenistic and Modern Culture

B
528
.C43
- 1980

Library of Congress Cataloging in Publication Data

Center for Hermeneutical Studies in Hellenistic and
    Modern Culture.
    Soul and body in stoicism.

    (Protocol series of the colloquies of the center ;
36 ISSN 0098-0900)
    Bibliography: p. 39-40
    1. Stoics--Congresses. 2. Soul--Congresses.
3. Body, Human--Congresses. I. Long, A. A.
II. Title. III. Series: Center for Hermeneutical
Studies in Hellenistic and Modern Culture. Protocol
series of the colloquies ; 36.
B528.C43 1980   128'.1   80-22935
ISBN 0-89242-035-9

Published by

The CENTER FOR HERMENEUTICAL STUDIES in
Hellenistic and Modern Culture

2465 Le Conte Avenue

Berkeley, CA   94709

USA

TABLE OF CONTENTS

SOUL AND BODY IN STOICISM[1]

Anthony A. Long

I. The Mind (Soul) Body Relationship and Greek Philosophy

What a modern philosopher might call problems of the self and problems of personal identity take the form, in Greek philosophy, of questions about the human *psyche* and its relation to the body. In this paper I propose to explore some of the ways in which the early Stoics approached such questions. The scholarly literature has not neglected the Stoic concept of *psyche*, but most of the discussion has focused upon detailed questions concerning the soul itself rather than its relationship to the body.[2] My procedure here will be designed primarily to illuminate that relationship. So, in the second part of the paper, I will discuss the Stoic concept of 'unified bodies;' I will then bring *psyche* more fully into the argument by considering the nature of animal bodies and psychic functions; and finally I will make some brief remarks about 'rational souls' and their relation to (their) bodies.

For reasons that should become clear it is peculiarly difficult to characterise the Stoic position on the relationship between soul and body. But it may be helpful, as an introduction, to make some comparisons with the principal rival accounts that we have from antiquity, the Platonic, Aristotelian, and Epicurean. If one were to draw up a table or questionnaire and consider the similarities and differences among these four positions, the two extremes would be represented by Plato on one side and Epicurus on the other. Broadly speaking, one may call Plato a dualist and Epicurus a materialist. Plato and Epicurus are diametrically opposed on the question of the soul's relation to the body. Thus (1), Plato allows that Socrates, or Socrates' soul, can exist without the body that Socrates now happens to have. But Epicurus maintains (2): Socrates, or Socrates' soul, cannot exist independently of just that body which is Socrates' body. (3) According to Plato, Socrates, or Socrates' soul, is an incorporeal substance which can exist independently of any body. (4) Epicurus holds on the other hand that Socrates is an arrangement of indivisible bodies (atoms), some of which constitute his flesh, blood, and bones, while others account for the life and other vital powers of that body. (5) For Plato Socrates, or Socrates' soul, is immortal. (6) But in the view of Epicurus Socrates is necessarily mortal, and his soul cannot survive the destruction of his body.

---

[1] An earlier version of this paper was presented to the Princeton University Ancient Philosophy Colloquium, in December 1978, which had the theme 'Mind and Body in Ancient Philosophy.' I am grateful for the comments that were made then, especially those by Professor Josiah B. Gould, the commentator on the paper. For the leisure to work on the subject I am greatly indebted to Princeton University which elected me a Senior Fellow of the Council for the Humanities for the first semester of 1978-79, and to the Institute for Advanced Study, Princeton, of which I was privileged to be a member during the second semester.

[2] H. von Arnim, *Stoicorum Veterum Fragmenta* (= *SVF*) II 217-235, gives the fullest collection of evidence for *anima hominis* in Stoicism prior to Panaetius. Many texts in other sections of his vols. I-III provide further material (cf. the Index vol. IV), but this collection here, as elsewhere, is far from complete. In this paper I shall be concerned with later Stoicism (Panaetius onwards) only incidentally. The most extensive modern treatment of the material is by Adolf Bonhöffer, *Epictet und die Stoa*, whose entire book, from pp. 29ff., is a detailed discussion of evidence on 'anthropology and psychology' from early Stoicism as well as Epictetus. Briefer accounts, from a variety of perspectives, may be found in the books by Bréhier, Gould, Long, Pohlenz, Rist, Sandbach, and Watson (the bibliographical references are given at the end of the paper).

The Aristotelian and Stoic accounts, which are harder to describe briefly, fall between these two extremes. Aristotle's notion, of the *psyche* as the 'form (or actuality) of a natural body which has life potentially,' has proved attractive to some contemporary philosophers because it seems to them to avoid the pitfalls of dualism and materialism.[3] Certainly, if we ignore the status and duration of 'the active intellect,' Aristotle seems to side with Epicurus at (2) and (6) above; for, if having a soul is to be an actually living body, it makes no sense to ask whether that form or actuality can exist without the body of which it is the form or actuality. But there is little justification for treating Aristotle's psychology as a whole as if the 'active intellect' were only an embarrassing appendage. The 'active intellect' has no corresponding bodily potentiality, and it is explicitly said to be 'what it is only when separated, and this alone is immortal and eternal,' *De an.* 3.5, 430a22-23. Aristotle's account is most safely regarded as sui generis with some dualist and some materialist features.

It is rather the same, though for different reasons, with the Stoics. Unlike Epicurus, and Aristotle (without the active intellect), they would not accept (2) and (6) above. They would say that Socrates' soul, though not immortal, could and would survive the destruction of his body and thus it can exist independently of that body.[4] In this respect they resemble Plato. But against Plato they defend a version of (4) whereby Socrates here and now is entirely an arrangement of two bodies, one answering to body in the ordinary sense and the other to life as a rational being. If then it is helpful to speak of dualism in Stoicism it is not a dualism of matter and incorporeal substance. For, given Stoic ontology, nothing can be truly predicated of Socrates which does not make reference to corporeal existence. In this respect the Stoics are at one with Epicurus. But at many points details of their position recall Aristotle so closely that we have reason to suspect his influence, an awareness of common problems, and Stoic attempts to improve upon him.

There is of course much common ground among all four philosophers. All of them accept the legitimacy of making a distinction between body and soul such that soul is the cause of intelligent life occurring within that part of space which is bounded by a normal human body. They all agree too in identifying the location of the principal activity of the soul with a particular region of the body.[5] What today would be called mental and moral attributes are universally regarded as attributes of the *psyche* as distinct from the body associated with that *psyche*; and to this extent notions such as personal identity and personality are 'psychic' rather than 'somatic;' which is not to say that they are uninfluenced or unmodified by the body's condition. Here there is room for considerable variation. It was also agreed, by all except the early Stoics, that the human soul itself admitted of a distinction between 'rational' and 'irrational' activities or

---

[3]This point is well brought out in Bernard Williams' paper 'Hylomorphism,' which he read to the Princeton colloquium (see n. 1 above). Two studies which illustrate Aristotle's apparent attractions are Jonathan Barnes, 'Aristotle's Concept of Mind,' *Pro. Aristot. Soc.* 72 (1971-2) 101-114 and H.M. Robinson, 'Mind and Body in Aristotle,' *CQ* NS 28 (1978) 105-124, which gives references to many recent discussions of Aristotle's psychology. See also the stimulating and provocative book by Edwin Hartman.

[4]The evidence on the soul's survival is well discussed by Hoven, who shows that probably all the leading Stoics posited survival of limited duration. The doctrine of periodic *ekpyrosis* and reconstitution of the universe excludes any straightforward notion of immortality.

[5]The Stoic *hegemonikon*, 'the principal part of the soul,' is situated in the heart which is also the primary location of the soul according to Aristotle in several different contexts; cf. Edwin Hartman 138f. For the Epicureans the *animus*, as distinct from the subordinate and pervasive *anima, media regione in pectoris haeret* (Lucret. 3.140). In the *Timaeus* Plato localizes 'the immortal reason in the head, the spirited part between the neck and the diaphragm, and the appetitive part in the belly (69d6 ff.),' T.M. Robinson, *Plato's Psychology* 106.

states of consciousness. All except the Epicureans extended the possession of soul beyond terrestrial creatures and traditional gods. The entire Stoic universe is an instance of the relation between body and soul; in Plato and Aristotle too the heavenly bodies are 'ensouled.'

II. The Soul and 'Unified Bodies'

If a modern philosopher claims that persons or human selves are bodies we naturally take him to be denying dualism or the Cartesian concept of mind. Persons in Stoicism are bodies, but this statement by itself does not make the Stoics *materialists as distinct from dualists*. The Stoics had reasons, as we shall see, for insisting that the soul is corporeal; but those reasons fall within a general conceptual framework which denies that anything can exist which is not a body or the state of a body. Since persons do exist they must be bodies, according to Stoicism. The corporeality of the soul is not simply an empirical truth in Stoicism, though empirical reasons were given in its favour. It is analytically or logically necessary that the soul be a body, given the Stoic conception of reality. Accordingly the corporeality of the Stoic soul becomes an informative notion only when we ask what kind of a body, or real thing , it is taken to be, rather than by contrasting it with the Platonic or Cartesian conception of an incorporeal soul or self.

A human being, in Stoicism, is a composite of a body, in the ordinary sense of body, and a *psyche* which is a body in some other sense.[6] More specifically he is an ensouled, rational, and mortal body. More basically he is a part of the universal stock of matter (*hyle*) pervaded through and through by a part of god (*theos*); or alternatively, he is a part of god pervading some part of the universal stock of matter. This last description of human beings is not, by itself, any ground for them to congratulate themselves on a special association with divinity. All things in the Stoic universe are combinations of god and matter, stones no less than men. But if god and matter in association fail to tell us what is human about persons, that is no cause for immediate alarm. The Stoic god, in its constant conjunction with matter, can make rational beings as well as stones. But it is worth dwelling, initially, on the fact that persons are not different from any other discrete objects in their basic principles or constituents. Men no less than stones are subject to the laws of physics; they resist and offer resistance to other discrete objects, just like stones; men and stones are alike in having a shape and identity which persists over time. There is in Stoicism a great chain of being which tolerates no discontinuity or introduction of principles which operate at one level but not at another. The entire universe is a combination of god and matter, and what applies to the whole applies to any one of its identifiable parts.

But to speak of god and matter in conjunction is somewhat abstract for present Stoic purposes. God and matter are the fundamental Stoic *archai*--active and passive principles--but they are never found in dissociation from one another.[7] Even in the simplest state of the universe, before any cosmic cycle has commenced, something can be predicated of matter, namely fieriness. God always causes matter to possess at least this quality. Nor can god act without matter to act upon. The conjunction of god and matter always results in qualified matter (hence the possible description of god as 'matter in a certain state').[8] God and matter together constitute something that not only

---

[6]A selection of texts: *bonum hominis necesse est corpus sit, cum ipse sit corporalis*, Sen. *Ep.* 106 = *SVF* 3.84, line 40; an 'animal' is οὐσία ἔμψυχος αἰσθητική, Diog. aert. 7.143 = *SVF* 2.633; ἐκ ψυχῆς καὶ σώματος συνέστηκεν (sc. ἄνθρωπος), Sextus Emp. *dv. math.* 11.46 = *SVF* 3.96; the upshot of Philo's classification at *SVF* 2.182 is man as body with soul, rational, and mortal.'

[7]On the *archai* see especially Lapidge, and Sandbach, 71-75.

[8]Some descriptions of god in relation to matter: 'matter is contemporaneous with god;' god is 'the power which moves matter;' god 'pervades matter;' god 'is mixed with

has mass or resistance to pressure, and that is extended in space, but something which has shape or form. Whether or not god and matter can, each by itself, be properly called bodies (as in the evidence they often are), it is certainly the Stoic view that every discrete body is matter pervaded and informed by god, and that each of these is necessary to its existence as a discrete body. The Stoics often described god as 'fire the craftsman' or as 'intelligent breath' (*pneuma*).[9] They also contrasted with the active principle thus described so-called 'inert elements,' earth and water. Even though any one of these active or passive elements must itself, in the most basic analysis, be a combination of matter and god, it will be correct and helpful, for my present purposes, to speak as though god is coextensive with *pneuma* and matter coextensive with the minimally qualified inert elements.

The justification for so doing is that the Stoics conceived wateriness and earthiness as 'transformations of fire' (or *pneuma*), and as such they are not instantiations of god *in propria persona*. The first order distinction between god and matter gives rise to a second-order distinction between a rarefied active body, which is the nearest thing possible to pure god, and a dense passive body, which is the nearest thing possible to unformed matter. The distinction between body and soul, and the distinction between all attributes or sets of things, are ultimately referable to the protean qualifications with which god informs matter.

This brief outline of the Stoic *archai* may help us to approach the question, is a man or an animal in Stoicism one body or two bodies?[10] The Stoics distinguished three kinds of bodies, or perhaps more accurately, four kinds, the fourth being a subdivision of the third: bodies composed of separated parts (*diestota*), such as an army; bodies composed of contiguous parts (*sunaptomena*), such as a house or a ship; unified bodies (*henomena*), such as stones and logs; and fourthly, or a subdivision of the last category, bodies unified and grown together, namely, living things (presumably including plants) (*SVF* 2.366 and 368 cf. *SVF* 2.1013). 'Grown together' (*sumphues*) is needed in addition to 'unified' to classify living bodies. Unity by itself does not point to life, any more than disjoined parts of an army signify something lifeless. Stones are like men in being 'unified' bodies, and their unity is due to the same cause. Both stones and men are 'held together' by the *pneuma* which pervades all the rest of their matter. Stones are said to be held together or controlled by (or participate in) 'mere *hexis*' or '*hexis* alone' (*SVF* 2.988, 1013, 714), where their *hexis* consists in 'cohesive *pneuma*' or '*pneuma* that turns back to itself' (*SVF* 2.368, 458). Animals in general in as much as they are 'unified bodies' are also said in one text to be 'governed by a single *hexis*' (*SVF* 2.1013). But men and animals in our evidence are generally differentiated from inanimate substances, such as stones, by reference to soul. We see that the breath of god moves in different ways. In the stone it is mere coherence (*hexis*) but in the animal it is soul.

We shall need to ask whether the Stoics thought that animals participate in *hexis* as well as soul, or whether the soul univocally accounts for those features of animals (bones and sinews) which are analogous to the coherence of stones. A related point, of

matter' or 'is in matter' or 'shapes each thing through the whole of matter' or 'is quality inseparable from matter' or 'is *logos* in matter': cf. von Arnim *SVF* vol. IV (Adler) s.v. θεός.

[9]E.g. Aetius *SVF* 2.1027; Alex. Aphr. *SVF* 2.310.

[10]For the question note also Plutarch's interpretation of the doctrine that 'each of us is two *hupokeimena*,' one *ousia*, the other *qualified* (supplying *poion* with Zeller), *Comm. not.* 1083C = *SVF* 2.762 with commentary by Harold Cherniss in Plutarch, *Moralia* XII part 2 (Loeb ed.) ad loc., and Dexippus *in Aristot. Cat.* p. 23,25 Busse = *SVF* 2.374. The passage needs detailed discussion, but the doctrine seems to me correctly understood by Dexippus as drawing a distinction between 'unqualified matter' (*ousia*) and 'individuating form' (e.g. Socrates)--i.e., in terms of the basic *archai*,--*hyle* and *theos*.

which I will give notice now, concerns plants. Stoic plants, unlike Aristotelian ones, do not have soul. Their powers of growth and reproduction are explained by *pneuma* which manifests itself as *physis* ('growth'/'nature'), a principle distinct both from bare *hexis* and also from soul (*SVF* 2.714-718). So the question arises of how functions of plants which animals also possess are analysed. Is *physis* a principle of life in the animal in addition to soul, accounting for its vegetative functions, or does the animal soul subsume the work of *physis* and account for everything that makes the body coherent and alive? Answers to these questions partly depend upon more basic interpretation concerning the concept of any 'unified body.'

The unity of any 'unified body,' be it a stone, plant, animal, or human being, is explicitly attributed not to the form or arrangement or inseparability of its parts, etc., but to one of its corporeal constituents, *pneuma*, and the 'cohesion' of 'tensional movement' this establishes throughout all the rest of the body. More particularly, the unity of all 'unified bodies' consists in the fact that they are instances of 'complete blending' (κρᾶσις δι' ὅλων); this technical expression refers to a form of compounding whereby 'two or even more bodies are extended through one another as wholes through wholes, in such a way that each of them preserves its own substance and qualities in a mixture of this kind ... For it is the special feature of things which are blended that they can be separated again from one another; and this can only take place if the things blended preserve their own natures in the mixture.'[11] Alexander of Aphrodisias, the source of this quotation or paraphrase of Chrysippus, observes that the Stoics cited the relation of soul and body as 'clear evidence' for such a kind of mixture: 'for none of the soul lacks a share in the body which possesses the soul. It is just the same too with the *physis* of plants, and also with the *hexis* in things which are held together by *hexis*. Moreover they say that fire passes as a whole through iron as a whole, while each of them preserves its own *ousia*.'[12] Alexander concludes this survey with the most general example of 'complete blending;' what is true of the unified bodies just considered is true a fortiori of the elemental relation between the fine active pair of elements, fire and air (= *pneuma*), and the dense passive pair, earth and water. Fire and air wholly pervade the passive elements, but all four of them preserve 'their own nature and coherence.'[13]

It follows from this account that the soul/body relationship is no more than one instance of a general principle in Stoic physics. It also follows that all so-called *unified bodies* are two bodies, two independent substances: to be a *unified body* is to consist of two separately identifiable and separable bodies which are so blended that you cannot take a part of one of them, however small, without also, in that process, making a part of the other(s).[14] The unity of a unified body accordingly is a function of 'complete blending.'

But how are we to understand this notion with reference to the relationship of the soul and the body? What is a human body in Stoicism when considered independently of the soul? We may clarify these questions by considering three possible answers.

1. *The body is the structure of bones, organs, blood, and skin which contains the soul and which the soul, in turn, pervades.* This is the straightforward answer, but it can scarcely be correct in this formulation. For the body, as so described, has a definite

---

[11]Alex. Aphr. *Mixt*. p. 216.28-31 Bruns = *SVF* 2.473 p. 154.22-25. For detailed discussion of this doctrine cf. Todd, 29-73.

[12]*Mixt*. p. 217.32-218.2 Bruns = *SVF* 2.473 p. 155.24-32. Todd, 119, translates the first sentence in my quotation marks, 'for there is nothing in the body possessing the soul that does not partake of the soul' (οὐδὲν γὰρ ψυχῆς ἄμοιρον τοῦ τὴν ψυχὴν ἔχοντος σώματος). But word-order and the train of thought make it preferable to take οὐδὲν ψυχῆς as the object of the sentence.

[13]*Mixt*. p. 218.2-6 Bruns = *SVF* 2.473.p. 155.32-36.

[14]Matter, according to Chrysippus, is infinitely divisible, Diog. Laert. 7.150 = *SVF* 2.482, as the doctrine of total blending requires, cf. Todd, 205ff.

complex structure: this means, according to Stoic metaphysics, that the body is already an instance of 'complete blending,' a compound structure generated by the interaction of *pneuma* and matter. But *pneuma* is the stuff of soul, and there is evidence that the Stoics supposed such bodily structures as bones to be due to the soul.[15] The body moreover is the body *of a living thing*. If then we take the body in this way it appears that we are already invoking the concept of soul; we do not have an independently identifiable substance answering to body.[16] But this is what the soul/body relationship, as a mixture, requires.

    2. *The body is matter in the form of earth and water*. This answer avoids the main difficulty in the previous one. Earth and water are not constituents of the soul, and so they are separately identifiable apart from soul. Moreover these dense elements do provide most if not all the material of which the body consists. But this answer raises new problems. It seems to be simply false, or at least quite uninformative, to say that an animal's or a man's body just is earth and water. Granted, the Stoics must regard a man, like any other unified body, as a compound of the active shaping principle (*logos* = god = *pneuma*) and the passive material principle (*hyle* = earth and water). But that analysis is at a level of such utter generality that it seems quite inadequate to make a helpful distinction between the animal or human soul and the animal or human body. It is not earth and water without qualification that might serve to identify a living thing's body, but earth and water in a certain form. Yet that brings us back to the problems of the first answer.

    3. *The body is earth and water informed by cohesive and vegetative (soul) pneuma, but not specific soul pneuma*. This third answer is a compromise between the two previous ones which seeks to keep their virtues and avoid their difficulties. I shall argue that it probably expresses the essentials of Chrysippus' position.

    According to Sextus Empiricus some Stoics distinguished two usages of the term *psyche*: they applied it quite generally to 'that which holds together the whole compound,' and specifically they used it to refer to the *hegemonikon* (*Adv. math.* 7.234). For these Stoics, Sextus continues, it is only the soul in the latter sense which is invoked *when we say that man is composed of body and soul*, or that death is the separation of soul from body. This last point seems to recognize the difficulty of the first answer I considered above. Soul in the sense, 'that which holds together the whole compound,' rules out any clear distinction between soul and body. Even a corpse, and all the more so a skeleton, possesses coherence over time. So a more specific usage of soul is required to justify speaking of a man as a compound of body and soul, or to explain death as their separation.

    The same distinction between two senses of soul is implied in a passage of Diogenes Laertius (7.138-9). Referring to books by Chrysippus and Posidonius he observes that *nous* pervades every part of the cosmos, just as soul (pervades every part) in us. 'But through some parts it is more pervasive and through others less so; for it passes through some parts as *hexis*, as through the bones and sinews; but through others as *nous*, as through the *hegemonikon*.' The basis of this distinction is of course the Stoic concept of *pneuma* and the different degrees of tension which characterise its movement. Since the soul itself is *pneuma*, and since *hexis* and *nous* are both functions of *pneuma* at different degrees of tension, it was possible for the Stoics to make soul responsible both for the form of the body (bones and sinews etc.) and for specifically psychic attributes. But they could only do so by distinguishing the soul as *hexis* (and, as we shall see later, *physis*) from the soul in the specific sense.

    I conclude therefore that the Stoics must invoke the concept of soul in order to account for an animal body as an identifiable substance. But this is not open to the objections of our first answer, once we cease to treat soul as a univocal concept. *Soul*

---

[15]This will be cited below, and cf. Posidonius F28ab Edelstein-Kidd for *psychichon pneuma* in bones.

[16]For an illuminating discussion of this kind of difficulty, cf. J.L. Ackrill 129-'

in general is responsible both for the body's form and for all vital functions. But we can mark off the body from the soul by distinguishing between bones and sinews (which are due to soul as *hexis*) and specifically psychic attributes (which are due to soul as *hegemonikon*). Thus both the body and the psychic attributes are matter in a certain state. But the nature of that 'certain state' depends upon the tension of the soul *pneuma*.

The point of decisive importance which will emerge more clearly as I proceed is the Stoics' concentration on the specific usage of soul, the soul as *hegemonikon*. It is not the soul as *hexis* which differentiates an animal from a stone, for a stone too is governed by *hexis*. That common pneumatic function indicates that both animals and stones have durable and individually identifiable bodies. It does not indicate that stones are in some peculiar sense alive, nor does it imply that an animal's bones and sinews are psychic attributes. But bones and sinews are, for excellent reasons, attributed to the working of soul at the most general level. An animal requires bones and sinews in order to live. The coherence of a stone has nothing to do with life. Therefore the *hexis* of stones is not a function of *pneuma* as soul, but the *hexis* of an animal must be due to soul. This makes it clear that an animal's body is *matter which has a form suitable for life*. I shall try to show in the next section how the Stoics drew on the two conceptions of soul--the general and the specific--in their account of the evolution of life in individual animals.[17]

III. The Soul and Animal Bodies

Having now clarified the Stoic distinction between the body and the soul we may now return to the question of their relationship, bearing the following points in mind: we are asking about the relationship between the body as an organic structure (held together by psychic *pneuma* in one sense of this expression) and the soul in its specific sense as *hegemonikon* (plus seven subordinate parts, see below p. 12), or principle of specifically animal life; we already know that they must be related to one another as constituents of 'total blending,' and that, accordingly, each of them has its own persisting substance; we also know (I think) that the soul, even in this specific sense, completely pervades all parts of the body, or at least, all parts where it is not already present as the principle of bodily form and coherence (*hexis*). In answer to the earlier question then, it seems to follow that all Stoic animals (things with soul) do consist of two bodies. They are compounds of what I shall call a flesh and bones body and a specific soul body. The specific soul body acts upon the flesh and bones body to make the compound of them both a sentient and self-moving being. The flesh and bones body contains the specific soul body and provides it with the bodily organs necessary for endowing the compound--the 'unified body'--with life as a sentient and self-moving being. From here onwards I shall conform with normal Stoic practice in using 'soul' to refer to soul in the specific sense.

[17]I cannot attempt to offer here a comprehensive survey of existing treatments of the Stoic concept of soul, but to the best of my knowledge, the problem of identifying the body and distinguishing between the two senses of soul has not been clearly recognised before (and I myself skated over it in *Hellenistic Philosophy* 171-172). For instance, R.D. Hicks 61 wrote: 'Soul is the unifying principle which holds the organic body together. It is diffused all over the body, since sensation can be localised at any point of the periphery.' The second sentence refers to the soul as the specific principle, in the unified animal body, which accounts for *aisthesis*. The first sentence looks as if it leads on to this; but, though Hicks does not say so, it should be related to the concept of soul as general principle of an animal's coherence. Bonhöffer is exceptional in recording the distinction between the two senses of soul, 105-106, but in my opinion he fails to see its point. He treats the 'soul which holds the whole compound together' as the *hegemonikon* and seven subordinate parts. But these, as we shall see, seem to have nothing to do with explaining the form of bodily parts such as bones and sinews. For some analogous difficulties in Aristotle, cf. Suzanne Mansion.

The Stoics argued formally for the corporeality of the soul; and the premises of their arguments help to show how they interpreted the relationship between soul and body. Three principal arguments are attested, which I will call respectively, genetic, sympathetic, and contactual. The genetic argument, attributed to Cleanthes, rests on the premises first that offspring of animals resemble their parents not only in respect of bodily attributes but also in respect of the soul, where soul refers to passions, character, mental dispositions; secondly, resemblance and lack of resemblance are predicated of body, and not of incorporeal.[18] Cleanthes' second argument is based on *sumpatheia*: 'nothing incorporeal shares in the suffering of a body, nor does a body share in the suffering of an incorporeal; but soul suffers with the body when the body is sick and being cut, and the body suffers with the soul; the body turns red when the soul is ashamed and pale when the soul is afraid. Therefore the soul is a body.'[19] Aristotle of course instanced the same phenomena in arguing that anger, fear, etc., though *pathe* of the soul, are 'inseparable from the physical matter of the animals' (*De an.* 403b17), but he did not conclude that the soul as such must be a body. The third argument, 'the contactual' one, has its fullest form in Chrysippus: 'Death is separation of soul from body; but nothing incorporeal is separated from body; for an incorporeal does not even make contact with a body; but the soul both makes contact with, and is separated from, the body; therefore the soul is a body.'[20]

All three arguments assume that there must be a relationship of physical contact between the flesh and bones body and that within the body in respect of which an animal has sensations. So why not say that the soul is a part of the flesh and bones body-- that sensation generally, and psychic attributes specifically, are nothing more than functions of the heart or the brain? The Stoics will not do this. They are willing to say that the soul is a physical part of the animal. But it is not a part or an organ of the flesh and bones body. The soul is a substance in its own right which permeates the flesh and bones body, and which leaves that body at death.[21]

The Stoics adopted this position, I suggest, not unthinkingly, nor out of respect for traditional Greek views or their own metaphysical assumptions. They supposed that an animal needs a body which is completely equipped with all the organs and functions of a flesh and bones body before its soul can come into existence, as the principle of specifically animal life for that flesh and bones body.

The soul cannot be an organ of the flesh and bones body because all bodily organs exist *before* the soul comes into being. The seed in semen, like soul, consists of 'hot breath' which 'moves itself;'[22] but the embryo which grows by the agency of this *pneuma* is not yet a *zoon*, an animal.' Throughout gestation the seed *pneuma* 'remains *physis*.'[23] This means that an embryo belongs to the biological category of plants. Its mode of

---

[18]Nemesius *Nat. hom.* p. 32 Matthaei = *SVF* 1.518, p. 117.7-11, with the same argument attributed to him in Tertullian, *De an.* 25 = *SVF* ad loc. The force of Cleanthes' second premise is obscure to me, since there seems no reason why two 'incorporeals' (*asomata*)--e.g. in Stoicism, two equivalent or contrary statements--cannot be described as 'like or unlike' each other respectively.

[19]Nemesius loc. cit. = *SVF* 1.518, p. 117.11-14.

[20]Nemesius *Nat. hom.* p. 53 = *SVF* 2.790, p. 219.24-28.

[21]'*Psyche* is a living creature; for it is alive and sentient' (βούλονται δὲ καὶ τὴ ἐν ἡμῖν ψυχὴν ζῷον εἶναι· ζῆν τε γὰρ καὶ αἰσθάνεσθαι) Stobaeus *Ecl.* 2 p. 65.1 Wachsmuth = *SVF* 3.306. The human soul is an offshoot (*apospasma*) of the cosmos *qua living creature*, Diog. Laert. 7.143 = *SVF* 2.633, cf. Diog. Laert. 7.156 = *SVF* 2.774, and for the soul's survival Hoven (n. 4 above).

[22]Cf. Diog. Laert. 7.158 = *SVF* 2.741, Galen *Def. med.* 94 vol. XIX Kühn p. 370 = *SVF* 2.742.

[23]Hierocles, ed. von Arnim col. 1.12-15.

existence is adequately identified by 'growth' (*physis*).[24] As gestation progresses the *physis pneuma* is said to become 'finer,' and at birth this *pneuma* 'changes into soul' (or '*animal*'),[25] as a result of being instantly hardened by contact with the cold air outside. Forgetting about the fantastic embryology we may note several further Stoic doctrines which well accord with this development from seed *pneuma* to soul *pneuma*. Like Aristotle they held that the heart is the first part of an animal to grow (Galen *SVF* 2.761) and that the heart in turn 'generates the other bodily parts.' The heart must own its origin to the activity of the seed *pneuma*; and when the soul itself is fully developed the left ventricle of the heart is full of soul *pneuma*.[26] So there is a continuing relationship between *pneuma* and the heart both before and after an animal's birth.

The evolution of life for a rational animal passes through three stages each of which is identified by changes to a persisting *pneuma*. The seed changes to *physis*, the *physis* to soul, and the soul eventually becomes a rational soul. The differences from Aristotle are interesting. A Stoic animal's capacity to grow and to feed (Aristotle's nutritive soul, apart from reproduction) is not, as I understand the evidence, attributable to soul in its specific sense. The soul in this sense is not responsible for the basic bodily functions, and as we shall see, all of its so-called 'functions' (*dunameis*) have to do with sentient life. The body's growth and nutritive powers are due to the causal presence of *pneuma*, but *pneuma* prior to its changing from *physis* to *psyche*. What then about these vital functions after birth? An animal has to feed and go on growing. Are we to say that when *physis* changes to soul the new soul inherits the functions of 'causing growth,' in addition to performing its work as the principle of sensation and locomotion? The evidence, mainly from Galen and Philo, does not support this. Galen, for instance, distinguishes three kinds of *pneuma*: *hektikon*, *physikon*, and *psychichon*, and says that it is the *physikon* which 'nurtures' animals and plants, and the *psychichon* which makes ensouled creatures sentient and capable of moving (*SVF* 2.716). Clement of Alexandria maintains that 'irrational animals' participate in *horme* and *phantasia* (i.e. psychic faculties) in addition to *hexis* and *physis* (*SVF* 2.714). Philo attributes bones to *hexis* and nails and hair to *physis* (*SVG* 2.458). Galen again says that 'every plant is directed by *physis*, and every animal by *physis* and *psyche* together; if at any rate all we men use the name *physis* for the cause of feeding and growth and such activities, and use *psyche* for the cause of sensation and self-movement' (*SVF* 2.718). These texts are all mutually consistent, and entitle us to conclude that the dominant Stoic doctrine distinguished the *pneuma* which changes from *physis* to soul from the *pneuma* responsible for bodily coherence and growth after an animal is born.

Since there is no good evidence that soul in the specific sense does control digestion, bodily growth, etc., we should probably conclude that the functions of the Aristotelian nutritive soul (apart from reproduction) become functions of the *body* when an animal is born.[27] The idea would be that the growth of the body is now such that the heart etc. can control purely bodily functions without needing direction from the soul

---

[24]Cf. Chrysippus ap. Plut. *Stoic. rep.* 1052F = *SVF* 2.806; Galen *De foet. form.* 3 vol. IV Kühn p. 665 = *SVF* 2.712.

[25]Hierocles col. 1.21-2 μεταβαλεῖν εἰς ψυχήν, with comments by von Arnim ad loc.; cf. Chrysippus ap. Plut. loc. cit., τὸ πνεῦμα μεταβάλλειν καὶ γίνεσθαι ζῷον.

[26]Galen *De plac.* I 6 p. 141 Müller = *SVF* 2.897 p. 246.12-14, cf. Gould, 126.

[27]Calcidius *Ad Tim.* 220 = *SVF* 2.879 p. 235.30-37 does appear to attribute to Chrysippus the doctrine that soul controls 'nutrition and growth' (*nutriendo*, *adolendo*, line 33 of the *SVF* text). But he does not show how this could be a function of any of the soul's eight parts; perhaps he has conflated soul in the specific sense with soul as *pneuma* in general.

(cf. *SVF* 2.708).[28] Presumably there must be *pneuma* of the *physis* tension within all bodily organs to maintain their form and functions, but this *pneuma* is no more part of the soul properly speaking than the *pneuma* which controls bones and sinews. Perhaps we can call it a persisting residue of the original *pneuma* which manufactured the living body.

The distinction between *physis* and *psyche* enabled the Stoics to unburden the soul from causing growth and nutrition; one can see why they want to do this. In the first place they need some way of distinguishing the flesh and bones body and its processes from mental functions. But, more importantly, they regarded the distinctive functions of animal life as sentience and locomotion.

Before discussing those functions I should like to compare the results of the last few pages with the conclusion of the second section of this paper. There is an apparent contradiction in the evidence, which my analysis reflects. Earlier we had a distinction between the soul as *hexis* accounting for bones and sinews (and bodily coherence generally), and the soul as specifically the *hegemonikon*, accounting for psychic attributes. Now, with the later evidence, an animal's coherence (*hexis*) and growth (*physis*) are not attributed to its soul at all. The animal's soul is a principle additional to, and subsequent upon, a coherent, growing organism. The problem is probably to be resolved by means of the original distinction I discussed between two senses of the word soul; an animal does not have two souls, but its single soul can be treated as either all of its *pneuma* or only the most tenuous parts of that substance, depending upon what questions we are asking. All of the *pneuma* is responsible for an animal's being the kind of body that animals are; so in that sense all the *pneuma* is the soul. But what differentiates an animal from a plant and a stone is that its growth and coherence are for the sake of living a sentient and mobile life. It is a life of at least that degree of complexity which characterises everything that has soul. So, in this sense, only the *pneuma* which makes an animal sentient, mobile etc., is the soul.

IV. Psychic Functions

We have seen the difficulty of making a distinction between the body of a living thing and its soul. But the Stoics were clearly on the right lines in using that hackneyed distinction for the important purpose of distinguishing between modes of life. Bodily processes are fundamental to an animal's life; but a different order of necessity is manifest in an animal's exercise of its senses. We speak unkindly but correctly of someone who has sustained gross and irreversible brain damage, but whose bodily functions can continue to be made to work, as living the life of a vegetable. What we mean is that such a person cannot live a human life, and has perhaps, even, ceased to be a person. There is something in favour then of using the distinction between body and soul to isolate, as the soul, those vital functions which most sharply mark off animals from plants. More particularly, the Stoics' specific concept of soul makes the point that bodily processes-- digestion and so forth--are not an animal's *governing principle*. What governs an animal, they said, is its soul, and that directs us to consider what an animal does, how it standardly behaves, as the key to understanding its nature.

The animal differs from the non-animal in respect of impression (*phantasia*) or sensation (*aisthesis*) and impulse (*horme*).[29] This is the standard Stoic view. Notice that these two functions of soul subsume Aristotle's *aisthetikon* and *kinetikon*. What it is to be a Stoic animal, most minimally, is to be a living body which is aware of itself and the external world, and more particularly, aware of itself reflexively as the subject and objec

---

[28]My interpretation thus differs sharply from the views of Bonhöffer 69 (cf. 105-106) and Pohlenz 87, who suppose that the soul which comes into being on an animal's birth takes over the functions of *hexis* and *physis*.

[29]Hierocles, col. 1.31-33; Philo *SVF* 2.844; Alex. Aphr. *SVF* 2.1002 etc.

of impulse. Awareness of, and impulse to pursue or avoid an external object, provide the necessary and sufficient conditions of animal locomotion. The fullest account of animal development is from the Stoic Hierocles, writing at the time of Trajan on the foundations of Stoic ethics.[30] He begins his discourse with embryology.

As soon as an animal is born, he argues, i.e. from the first moment that it has a soul, it has awareness of itself.[31] He advances a series of arguments to support this thesis in opposition to those who say *aisthesis* is just for recognizing 'externals.'[32] The first psychic action of an animal is *sunaisthesis* of the body's parts and functions.[33] Evidence for this is, for instance, that birds perceive that they have wings, humans perceive that they have sense organs and that each of these has its own function: seeing, hearing, etc.[34] Furthermore, animals are immediately aware of a means of defending themselves.[35] The mechanism which explains self-awareness appears to be 'tensional movement,' the concept which explains the stone's coherence and the plant's growth.[36] In the animal 'tensional movement' is (in addition) the soul's mode of action. Hierocles maintains that the soul, because it is mixed with all the parts of the flesh and blood body, acts upon and is acted upon by them: 'For the body, just like the soul, offers resistance (*antibatikon*). And the *pathos*, which is a case of their simultaneously pressing together and resisting each other, is generated. From the outermost parts inclining within, it travels to the *hegemonikon*, with the result that apprehension (*antilepsis*) takes place both of all the body's parts and those of the soul. This is equivalent to the animal's perceiving itself.'[37] It is tempting to take this passage as giving not the paradigm account of sense-perception or any specific psychic act, but quite generally, as a description of the minimal conditions of any moment of conscious life. Hierocles does not say or imply that the *pathos* which results from contact between body and soul must be a result of some specific event affecting body or soul. The mere fact that body and soul are in constant conjunction is perhaps sufficient to constitute awareness of *meself*, where 'oneself' equals a living body. But Hierocles' main purpose is to demonstrate that feelings and sensations are psychic events such that the subject of them is aware that it is *his* body which is affected.[38]

Self-awareness is not the only minimal condition of having a soul. Along with self-awareness goes *horme*, 'impulse,' which also has the animals' own *sustasis*, 'constitution,' as its primary object from birth. Hierocles and Seneca adduce evidence from the behaviour of animals in support of this claim, e.g. tortoises' efforts to turn themselves back on to their feet, and young children's attempts to stand, even though they keep

---

[30]Cf. von Arnim, *Hierokles Ethische Elementarlehre*, and S.G. Pembroke 118-119. Hierocles' account is more compendiously repeated in Cic. *Fin.* 3.16ff.; Aulus Gellius 12.5.7; Diog. Laert. 7.85-86, and with more detail in Seneca *Ep.* 121.

[31]Col. 1.37-39.

[32]Col. 1.44ff.

[33]Col. 1.51, col. 2.1-3.

[34]Col. 1.51-61.

[35]Col. 2.3ff.

[36]Col. 4.27-38 with von Arnim's commentary ad loc.

[37]Col. 4.44-53; for the text and bibliography, apart from von Arnim, cf. Pembroke 132 n. 22.

[38]I think this may include all that is meant by 'apprehension of all the soul's parts' (end of quotation in main text). But others have distinguished the soul's consciousness of itself from its consciousness of the body, cf. von Arnim *Hierokles* xxviviii; Pembroke 119.

falling down, are not due to a desire to escape pain, but a desire to be in that state which they are conscious of as their own (natural) constitution.[39] An animal does not know *quid sit animal, animal esse se sentit* (Sen. *Ep.* 121.11).

The Stoics' emphasis on self-consciousness is quaint, especially if we think of animals as Cartesian automata. But there is of course a problem about denying it. For we surely do want to say that animals see things and feel pain, and if an animal sees things and feels pain then some value must be assigned to the 'it' which sees and feels. If an animal does not in some sense experience itself as the locus of its seeing and feeling then we must surely deny that seeing and feeling can be predicated of it. What the analysis of such a self can be it is naturally impossible to give in any but the most elementary terms. The Stoics insist most strongly that animals are 'not rational' (*aloga*). They lack the distinctively human quality of soul, but this quality is regarded as a modification of the minimal soul, something which gradually develops in the human infant out of the faculties which men and animals share.

We should not then think of rationality as an additional 'part' of the Stoic soul. All mortal animals have the same eight psychic parts. The soul of all animals is an *aisthetike anathumiasis*--an exhalation of breath capable of perceiving (*SVF* 1.141, 2.778), and this general definition seems to be consistent with its eight specific parts. Five of these are the five senses; the remainder are voice, reproduction, and the so-called *hegemonikon*.[40]

In dividing the soul into parts the Stoics were drawing attention to its diffusion throughout the body and its multiplicity of functions. But the partition of the soul is not similar to the Platonic model. What Plato distinguishes as reason, spirit, and appetite are, in the Stoic soul, all activities of the dominant part, the *hegemonikon*; the remaining seven parts, though physically attached to the *hegemonikon* seem to be purely the instruments of its activity. The Stoic soul is not fully analogous to the brain and the nervous system; but the relationship of the *hegemonikon* to the other seven parts is obviously comparable, both spatially and functionally, to the brain and the nerves which unite it with all parts of the body.

On this eight-part model, voice and reproduction resemble the five senses in being *pneumata* stretching from the *hegemonikon* to specific bodily organs. The counting of voice and reproduction as distinguishable parts of soul became controversial. Panaetius rejected it (fr. 36 van Straaten), but his claim that voice should be regarded as a 'movement in accordance with impulse,' and therefore a function of the *hegemonikon*, does not seem to differ substantially from the earlier position (cf. Diog. Laert.7.55). His predecessors also attributed voice to 'impulse,' in the case of irrational animals, or to 'thought' (rational impulse?) in the case of men; but they probably argued that though voice is a function of consciousness, the *hegemonikon* needs to attach itself to the larynx and the tongue, just as its activity in sense perception requires attachment to the sense organs.

They must also have been concerned to provide the human *hegemonikon*, which is totally *logikon*, with the instrument for rational discourse (thought). Reproduction looks more puzzling, but only if we associate it on Aristotelian lines with the nutritive soul, as Panaetius seems to have done in explaining it as part of *physis* (fr. 86 van Straaten). Earlier Stoics did not of course claim that life at every level can only be transmitted through the soul's activity (the seeds of plants do not require a soul). What they thought was probably that animals do not reproduce without sensing and wanting a sexual partner, and more important still perhaps, that the soul itself must control the production of seed or female fluid which is to be capable of generating offspring which themselves will have soul.

---

[39]Hierocles col. 7.5-10 (Pembroke n. 27, 143), Sen. *Ep.* 121.8, cf. Pembroke 119 with n. 28.

[40]For the evidence cf. *SVF* 2.823-33.

But the most interesting concept is the *hegemonikon* itself. I have mentioned its being located in the heart; just as the heart is said to be the source of other bodily parts, so probably the potential *hegemonikon's pneuma* in the embryo develops before the other parts of the soul, which are described as its 'offshoots' (*ekpephukota, SVF* 2.836). The nutriment of the soul is said to be blood (*SVF* 1.140), or 'the best blood' (*SVF* 2.781), with respiration also contributing (*SVF* 2.782-3). The Stoics grasped, however perversely, the vital relation between blood and respiration, and it is interesting that the soul's feeding requires an interaction between the heart and the *hegemonikon*. This also confirms the suggestion that nutrition in general is a function of the heart, not the soul, and it shows most plainly that the heart is the vital centre of an animal. Destroy the heart and you destroy both the soul's food supply and its principal location. The importance of the heart to the unity of the animal helps to explain Chrysippus' strenuous efforts to defend it as the seat of the soul.

This discussion of psychic functions has been but a glimpse of a very large subject. I hope it has served, however, to bring out some general points of interest. The Stoics' anatomical knowledge was extremely rudimentary; but their conception of body and soul as two independent things which are 'completely blended' clearly induced them to explore the relationship between bodily organs and the psychic functions they regarded as supremely explanatory in an animal's life. Body and soul come together, most significantly, in the heart; but although the same conjunction is characteristic throughout the entire animal, it remains no more than a conjunction. Body and soul are not two aspects of a single substance. They are separate substances.

The soul is not the activity of the heart; the heart is not the cause of the soul. Their relationship exemplifies the unity of an animal, but an animal's unity as a living thing depends on a partnership between two distinct bodies. The closer one of these bodies, the soul, becomes to cosmic *logos* = god, so much less does it have in common with flesh and bones. For a whole complex of reasons the Stoics want to emphasize the kinship between man and god. But they cannot do this, without weakening the connexion between body and soul. Paradoxically, it seems, animals turn out to be better examples of 'unified bodies' than persons. This will become clearer as we consider the similarities and differences between their souls.

V. The Rational Soul

No philosophers have emphasized more strongly than the Stoics did that rationality is *the* determinant of human life, and that it marks men off sharply from all other animals. And yet, as we have already seen, the human soul endows a human body with other psychic attributes which also belong to animals. This is not just a recognition of the uninteresting fact that men and animals alike can see, hear, etc. The human soul was conceived by the Stoics as something which has the same parts and functions as the animal soul. But what differentiates them is the presence or absence of *logos*: the growth and maturity of rationality are conceived as totally modifying the psychic parts and functions which, in themselves, are common to animals and men.

I think this point is established, or at least implied, by a seemingly authoritative text of Iamblichus. Writing of what must be the human *hegemonikon* he treats it as the common *substrate* of four 'specific qualities' (*SVF* 2.826). They are, in this order, *phantasia, sunkatathesis* (assent), *horme*, and *logos*. The oddity here is *logos*. It was basic Stoic doctrine that the entire human *hegemonikon* was rational, through and through, yet here *logos* is but the last member of a quartet. The reason for this, I suggest, is that the first three 'qualities' pick out permanent dispositions of any *hegemonikon*, animal or human. That is to say, the *hegemonikon* is involved in every action of the soul in at least one of these three ways. The soul's seeing or hearing is not something independent of the *hegemonikon*. It *is* the *hegemonikon*, in its function as *phastasia*, the awareness of sense objects, reported to it as changes to the sense organs. Frequently too the awareness of a sense object will also be experienced as a *horme* or *aphorme*, an impulse to pursue or avoid the external thing causing the stimulation of the sense organs. But such impulses will not serve as causes of action independently of 'assent,' the third of the soul's basic qualities or functions.

There seems no good reason to question those few texts (Nemesius and Alexander of Aphrodisias *SVF* 2.979, 991) which explicitly attribute 'assent' to all animals; and the treatment of assent as a quality or faculty which can be named *independently of logos* (in *SVF* 2.826 above) can best be explained on this assumption.[41] The assent of non-rational animals is presumably to be analysed as some kind of non-verbalized understanding or acceptance of the *phantasia* as a genuine awareness of an external object or bodily disturbance, which will give rise, often, to an impulse in accordance with the animals' *oikeiosis*. Hence perhaps remarks in Stoic texts that animals have *simile quiddam mentis, unde oriantur rerum adpetitus* (Cic. *ND* 2.29), and the 'potential reasoning' of Chrysippus' dialectical dog (Sextus Emp. *PH* 1.69).

If, as I suggest, any soul's activities consist in imaging, assenting, and impulsion, then imaging, assenting, and impulsion together pick out what it is to have a soul, or to be an animal.[42] This has interesting consequences for the soul of rational beings. *Logos* is something which develops gradually in the human soul. The soul of an infant has only potential *logos*, and its behaviour is governed by an as yet non-rational *horme*. Later '*logos* supervenes as the craftsman of impulse' (Diog. Laert. 7.86). The Stoic doctrine is not that *logos* comes into being as a new faculty to be set alongside impulse etc. What they claim rather is that the three psychic faculties which humans share with animals *all* become modified, in men, by *logos*. There is evidence to support this in Stoic terminology. Human *phantasiai* (referring to all of them) are *logikai*.[43] The *horme* of men is also qualified by the same adjective, *logike*.[44] As for the 'assent' of men, its proper object is *lekta*, whose connexion with *logos* needs no demonstration.[45] *Lekta* comprise, most importantly, the *meanings* of declarative sentences, alternatively called *axiomata*. *Noeseis*, 'acts of thinking,' are described as *logikai phantasiai* (Galen, *SVF* 2.89).

All of this proves that the *logos* of the human soul is not one faculty, among others, but the *mode* of the whole soul's operation. Like the animals, human beings are creatures whose psychic attributes and behaviour can be analysed in terms of the three faculties, imaging, assenting, and impulsion. But the human mode of imaging etc. is invariably a rational activity. There is another way of putting this which expresses, I think, the central insight of the Stoics: the human soul is a capacity for living as a language animal.[46] If I am right in my earlier interpretation of the soul in its

---

[41]Cf. also Cic. *Acad.* 2.37 where Lucullus, speaking for the Stoicizing Antiochus, claims that action, which distinguishes *animal* from *inanimum*, implies *sensus* and *adsensus*. I recognize that those who think assent must and can only be given to propositions may resist this claim. But the Stoics thought assent was given to *phantasiai* as well as to *axiomata*. Perhaps *oikeiosis* at all levels was thought to depend on assent, cf. Cic. *Acad.* 2.38; and, in general, *Hellenistic Philosophy* 172-173.

[42]'Imaging' is but one of many unsatisfactory renderings of *phantasia*. The noun expresses the state of 'being appeared to,' but a translation needs to be wide enough to accommodate mental as well as sense impressions.

[43]Diog. Laert. 7.51 = *SVF* 2.61, cf. G.B. Kerferd in *Les Stoiciens et leur logique* ed. J. Brunschwig (Paris 1978) 252-3, who has convinced me that I was wrong to argue in *Problems* 83 that some human *phantasiai* might not be *logikai*.

[44]Stobaeus *SVF* 3.169, cf. Diog. Laert. 7.86.

[45]Stobaeus *SVF* 3.171.

[46]I have explored the implications of this more fully elsewhere, *Problems* chapter V; *Hellenistic Philosophy* 123-125, 175-176, etc.

specific sense, then the human soul does not animate the body in its structure as flesh and bones. It turns that structure into an instrument for perception, judgement, and desire (here I refer again to the three psychic faculties), where all three of these, even when mediated by the senses, are 'rational,' in the sense that they belong to a creature whose life is irreducibly determined by its capacity to think and to talk.

A soul's rationality, it seems, is a cooperative development of 'voice' and 'impression' (*phone* and *phantasia*). Both of these provide ways of distinguishing rational from non-rational souls. Human *phone* is 'articulate;' it issues from the heart and *hegemonikon* and 'is despatched from thought.'[47] Human *phantasiai* differ from those of animals in being capable of 'combination and transference,' an obscure way of saying that human beings naturally make inferences and form concepts.[48] Language is the usage of significant sounds to express thoughts (*phantasiai*). But the expression of a thought in language is something *said* or *meant*, a *lekton*, which is incorporeal, an abstraction from body.[49]

I allude, quite baldly I fear, to the doctrine of *lekta* here because it may raise new questions about the relationship between human soul and human body. Animals according to the Stoics appear to be granted some form of self-consciousness, as we have seen, but *lekta* can have no part to play in the animal's psychology. Animals do not say anything, and so their image of themselves cannot be linguistic or conceptual. The object of animal awareness would seem to be exclusively its body and changes to its body. But the Stoics probably supposed that the human soul, regularly and naturally, reacts to and regulates the body by talking to itself; for this purpose it employs *lekta* which, so far from being reducible to body, are actually *incorporeal*. The human soul can describe its experience, and so it is not restricted to a uniform set of reactions to the body. It can literally govern the body because it can decide what description and value to give to its present, past, or future bodily states.[50]

There appears then to be something irreducibly mental about the human soul, and this is due to its linguistic consciousness. The Stoics do not deny a necessary interaction between bodily states and conditions of the soul; that would be both implausible and quite out of key with their conception of body and soul as 'totally blended.'[51] But I think they would say that no causal necessity links bodily changes and all of the soul's reaction to them. The soul has the capacity to give or withold its assent to judgements about the body's condition and needs. So, while Stoics would no doubt admit that the soul cannot fail to be aware of an empty stomach, they would deny that that awareness automatically triggers a desire to eat. The hunger sensation and the desire to eat are separate states of the soul. The former is an unavoidable psychic reaction to the body; but the latter depends on the soul and the judgement that the soul makes. We could say that it is a relation between the soul or person and a proposition.

Such a distinction between body and rational soul is fundamental to Stoic ethics. Speaking strictly the Stoics said that nothing good or bad can affect the body of a man; good or bad, in the strict sense, can only be predicated of states of the soul and actions which are defined by the state of a soul. This doctrine is not a denial of bodily pain or pleasure, much less a denial that men may judge bodily pains to be bad and

---

[47]Diog. Laert. 7.55 (Diogenes of Babylon) which is inconsistent with Sextus Emp. *Adv. math.* 8.276, where birds are said to utter 'articulate cries;' Galen *SVF* 3.894, quoting Chrysippus.

[48]Sextus Emp. *Adv. math.* 8.276, cf. *Problems* 87 with n. 54.

[49]Evidence and discussion in *Problems* 82-84.

[50]Animals have only a most rudimentary concept of time, Cic. *Off.* 1.11; Seneca *Ep.* 124.17.

[51]For useful discussions of the interaction cf. Lloyd 234ff. and Rist 37-53.

pleasures good. But the Stoics held that such judgements indicate a morally weak state of the soul since they confuse what is truly valuable (moral virtue) or harmful (moral weakness) with the condition of the body.

This attitude of emotional indifference to bodily pains and pleasures highlights the supposed independence and value of the soul. It explains the tendency to regard the humanity of a man, his real self, as identical to his *hegemonikon*. Cleanthes allegedly called man 'soul alone' (*SVF* 1.538), and Epictetus sometimes treats the body as the mere container of the 'divine' soul or the ego.[52]

The dualist strain becomes still more evident when one reflects on the physical differences and functions of flesh and bones body and rational soul. If the *pneuma* which animates a plant-like embryo must be greatly refined in order to change to an animal soul, so much finer must be the *pneuma* of the rational soul. In its relation to the divine essence the human soul is the most rarefied of all bodies. Does this perhaps help to explain how a rational soul, while remaining corporeal, can be conscious of the incorporeal *lekta*? At any rate, its capacity for abstract thought represents some kind of transcendence over the purely corporeal which strictly is the only kind of existence the Stoics recognized. When we recall that the *hegemonikon* is credited with limited survival in separation from the body, rising baloon-like from the corpse, the dualism and the separation of body from spirit become evident again.

So how are we to view soul and body in Stoicism? As I began by saying, their relationship is an instance of the universal principle of god pervading and giving form and energy to matter. The series, *hexis-physis*-soul-rational soul, gives us the means of classifying all 'unified bodies' as different manifestations of god's interaction with matter. But god is only represented *in propria persona* in the rational soul. Human beings share properties of stones, plants, and animals; what they share with stones and plants accounts respectively for their bodies as coherent, growing entities; what they share with animals, in addition, is the capacity to behave as conscious and self-conscious bodies, but the mode of all their consciousness is distinctively rational.

Physiologically speaking, human body and soul, during a person's existence, are interdependent and inseparable from one another. The body needs the soul in order to be a living *human* body; the soul needs the body, out of which it originally grows, as its location, partial source of energy (blood), and instrument for actualising consciousness. But the soul's activities as mind--perceiving, judging, desiring etc.--though dependent on the soul's relationship with the body, are not reducible to or equivalent to that relationship. Psychologically and morally speaking, persons for the Stoics are states of rational consciousness, or most literally and accurately, 'intelligent warm breaths,' which inhabit flesh and bones bodies, and use them as instruments for their own life.[53]

---

[52]Bonhöffer 29-30; see further Rist 256ff.

[53]The last pages of this essay only touch on a number of complex issues which need far more thorough treatment than I have given them. Another topic which requires proper discussion is the similarities and differences between Aristotelian and Stoic psychology (cf. Philippson); that too I have only been able to hint at.

BIBLIOGRAPHY

Arnim, H. von   *Stoicorum Veterum Fragmenta* (*SVF*)

------   *Hierokles. Ethische Elementarlehre* (Pap. 9780) Berliner Klassikertexte, Heft iv 1906

Ackrill, J.L.   'Aristotle's Definitions of *Psuche*,' *Proceedings of the Aristotelian Society* LXIII (1972-3) 119-133

Bonhöffer, A.   *Epictet und die Stoa* (Stuttgart 1890)

Bréhier, E.   *Chrysippe et l'ancien stoicisme*[2] (Paris 1951)

Gould, J.   *The Philosophy of Chrysippus* (Leiden 1970)

Hartman, E.   *Substance, Body, and Soul. Aristotelian Investigations* (Princeton 1977)

Hicks, R.D.   *Stoic and Epicurean* (New York 1910)

Hoven, R.   *Stoïcisme et stoïciens face au problème de l'au-delà* (Paris 1971)

Lapidge, M.   ''Αρχαί and στοιχεῖα: A Problem in Stoic Cosmology,' *Phronesis* 18 (1973)

Lloyd, A.C.   'Emotion and Decision in Stoic Psychology,' in *The Stoics*, ed. J.M. Rist (Berkeley and Los Angeles 1978) 233-46

Long, A.A., ed.   *Problems in Stoicism* (London 1971)

------   *Hellenistic Philosophy* (London 1974)

Mansion, S.   'Soul and Life in the *De anima*,' in *Aristotle on Mind and the Senses*, ed. G.E.R. Lloyd and G.E.L. Owen (Cambridge 1978)

Pembroke, S.G.   'Oikeiosis," in Long, *Problems* 114-149

Philippson, E.   'Zur Psychologie der Stoa,' *Rheinisches Museum* NS 86 (1937) 140-179

Pohlenz, M.   *Die Stoa*[4] (Göttingen 1970)

Rist, J.M.   *Stoic Philosophy* (Cambridge 1969)

Sandbach, F.H.   *The Stoics* (London 1975)

Todd, R.B.   *Alexander of Aphrodisias on Stoic Physics* (Leiden 1976)

Watson, G.   *The Stoic Theory of Knowledge* (Belfast 1966)

Response by John M. Dillon, Professor of Classics
University of California, Berkeley

Professor Long has performed a great service by his lucid discussion of the nature of the two essences, body and soul, upon whose 'total blending' the human person depends for its existence. I wish I had time to do more justice to his remarks, but I hope at least that the following notes may serve to contribute to the discussion.

1. There seems to be some semantic confusion among the Stoics between psyche as a term for all levels of *pneuma* that pervade a living body, including *hexis* and *physis*, and *psyche* proper, which is the sentient element, the *hegemonikon*, together with the five senses, and the faculties of generation and speech. This confusion they inherit, presumably, from Platonic and Aristotelian doctrine. When it comes down to it, though, the two substances involved in the 'total blending' are (1) body, plus what Aristotle would term the nutritive soul, and (2) soul, which is limited to the sentient and rational soul. This latter, it seems, can lead an independent existence after death for at least a limited time (cf. *SVF* II 809-22), and it is this doctrine and its implications to which I would like mainly to direct my remarks on the present occasion.

2. As Anthony Long presents the situation, the stone or plant, as opposed to the animal, irrational or rational, is one body rather than two--or do I misunderstand? *Hexis* and *physis* are characteristics of unified bodies, but do not themselves constitute 'bodies,' whereas *psyche* and *logike psyche* constitute separate bodies. It seems strange to me that irrational soul, even though it involves *synaisthesis*, *phantasia*, *horme*, and *synkatathesis*, should be any more a separate body than *physis*. It seems just a further development of *physis*. If it is a separate body, then it would seem logical that it should survive death, even if for a shorter time than a rational soul. Fido's soul should exist by itself for a few months, at least. But we learn from Arius Didymus (*SVF* II 809) that the souls of irrational animals perish with their bodies. This leaves it unclear, perhaps, whether the irrational soul is just a rather frail construction, or whether it is simply an aspect or state of the living body. I would assume the latter alternative.

3. Where, then, does one draw the line? The sources seem to make no distinction between the *hegemonikon* and the other seven parts of the souls of rational beings when talking of its survival after death. Arius Didymus (*loc.cit.*) tells us that the soul does not perish immediately after parting from the body, but lasts on by itself for certain lengths of time, the souls of the good (*spoudaioi*) lasting all the way to the *ecpyrosis*, the souls of the foolish (*aphrones*--the vast majority) for various limited times, presumably according to their degree of foolishness. I suppose that the length of survival of a rational soul after death is determined by the degree of coherence attained by that soul by the time of death, the coherence of the soul of the *spoudaios* being far greater than that of the others by reason of its excellent 'vibrations'.

4. But of this rational soul what really can be imagined to survive? Can we suppose that the five senses, the generative faculty and the faculty of speech, all somehow survive death, and maintain a spherical and pneumatic existence somewhere in the cosmos? This seems a little strange to me. The sense-faculties and the others cannot, surely, survive the loss of their appropriate organs. Presumably what happens is that the *hegemonikon* withdraws itself from these, even as it had extended itself into them originally like an octopus (*SVF* II 827), and it is essentially the *hegemonikon* that survives.

5. So how, in Anthony Long's words, *are* we to view soul and body in Stoicism? How different in fact is the Stoic doctrine of all soul, apart from the rational

hegemonikon, from that of Aristotle, apart from the Active Intellect? (I have been tempted to wonder sometimes if the A.I. isn't perhaps just the totality of the first principles of logical thought, mildly personified, but the less said of that, perhaps, the better.) Most soul, for the Stoics, sounds rather like the 'first entelechy of a body capable of having life,' does it not?

Response by G.B. Kerferd, Hulme Professor of Greek
University of Manchester, England

The whole paper seems to be both profoundly new and illuminating, and also in all essential matters absolutely sound, correct and not to be challenged in any way. For purposes of discussion I would like to concentrate attention on two main points, both of which are very much matters of presentation, and which are indeed considerably modified within the paper itself as its own argument develops. But despite this their importance perhaps justifies some comment.

On p.3 line 14 we are told that 'it is analytically or logically necessary that the soul be a body, given the Stoic conception of reality.' I think I understand the reason for this statement. For the Stoics, for anything to exist (in the full sense of existence) it must be a body. From this it follows that if the soul *exists* it must be a body. But it is wrong to state that for the Stoics it is analytically true that the soul is a body. This would imply that the Aristotelian doctrine of the soul as the form or actuality of a body was for the Stoics self-contradictory. But for the Stoics the Aristotelian doctrine would be simply to view the soul as a *sōma pōs echon*--the body in a certain condition and there is nothing self-contradictory for them about such a way of looking at things. Indeed they themselves regarded the soul as *pneuma pōs echon*, cf. *SVF* II 443, 806. *Pōs echon* is the third of the Stoic 'categories.' It has, it is true, actually been maintained (by O. Rieth, *Grundbegriffe der stoischen Ethik* [1933] 77-84) that the *Pōs echon* is itself material, producing a state in a second piece of matter by interpenetrating it. But the evidence against this is strong (see e.g. Long, *Problems* 53, *Hellenistic Philosophy* 162-163). The better view is that conditions (*Pōs echonta*) do not act on the qualified substrate, they are states of that entity. This, notwithstanding the fact that the second category, quality, probably *was* regarded as corporeal by the Stoics, being in fact the active principle at work on the passive. From this it follows that the Stoics could certainly contemplate the Aristotelian doctrine as something free from internal contradiction. Their reasons for rejecting it were different. They were in fact principally the three reasons excellently described on p.8, the "genetic," the "sympathetic" and above all the "contactual." But from this it follows that the Stoic reasons for asserting that the soul is a body were synthetic rather than analytic. This is in fact recognised on p.8 when we are told that the Stoic view of the soul-body relationship did not spring from "their own metaphysical assumptions."

On p.6 onwards the Stoics are credited with two senses of soul--soul as *hexis* and soul as *hegemonikon*. I am not satisfied that the early Stoics ever in fact spoke in this way, though Posidonius may have done so. On p.7 it is in fact conceded that in normal Stoic practice it is only in the second sense that the term soul is used. I would suspect that it was never in fact used by them in the first sense despite the unnamed 'others' in Sextus VII 234. Certainly the operational force here is always simply *Pneuma*. Not all *Pneuma* is however Soul for the Stoics, only *Pneuma pōs echon* cf. *SVF* II 443 and 806. A terminologically clear picture is given in *SVF* II 458 with 716 and 714. *Pneuma* holds together bodies such as stones in a *Hexis*. When such a *Hexis* is itself in a state of change or movement it constitutes *Physis*, as in plants. Soul is *Physis* with the addition of *Phantasia* and *Horme*, as in animals, and *Nous* or *Logikē Psychē* is found only in human beings (and gods). What is operating in each of these cases is however for the Stoics *Pneuma* and not *Soul* since *Soul* is confined to animals (rational and otherwise). The brilliant Stoic conception of a developing series of *Pneuma pōs echon* is convincingly expounded in Long's paper. And certainly this *Pneuma* interpenetrates the body which is alive by the same kind of penetration as occurs in the *Hexis* of inanimate objects such as stones. One may then ask whether it is different *Pneumata* or different pieces of *pneuma* that are responsible for the *Hexis* of e.g. bones (which are stone-like) and the *Physis* of hair and nails (which are plant-like in that they grow) and the *Psyche* found in the reception of *Phantasiai* and *Hormai*. A possible answer would be neither: it is simply the one, single *Pneuma* in varying states of tension. But as the variation must be in part simultaneous we perhaps have, after all, to accept some partition or internal distribution of the one *Pneuma* in order to explain our various "bodily" functions. Points that seem to me possibly to call for further investigation are (1) what extra degree of tension (if that is what it is) is involved in the transition from a simple (inanimate) unified body to a body which is both unified and "grown together," and (2) the question whether the relation of the *Pneuma* to the body is to be seen technically as a *Mixis* rather than a *Krasis* in the light of the distinctions drawn in *SVF* II 471 where *Krasis* seems to be confined to the putting together of *moist* bodies such as water and wine.

Response by David Winston, Professor of Hellenistic and Judaic Studies
Center for Judaic Studies, Graduate Theological Union

Professor Long's paper is a splendid analysis of the Stoic conception of the body-soul relationship, precise in its formulation and exceedingly clear in its presentation. My response will focus on parts II and III which deal with the soul's relationship to "unified bodies" and animal bodies. Long correctly points out that the Stoics must invoke the concept of soul in order to account for an animal body. He then goes on to argue that a Stoic animal's capacity to grow and to feed is not attributable to soul in its specific sense. When *physis* changes to soul, the new soul does not inherit the functions of causing growth, in addition to performing its work as the principle of sensation and locomotion.

Galen, for instance, distinguishes three kinds of *pneuma*: *hektikon, physikon,* and *psychikon*, and says that it is the *physikon* which nurtures animals and plants, and the *psychikon* which makes ensouled creatures sentient and capable of moving (*SVF* 2.716). Philo attributes bones to *hexis* and nails and hair to *physis* (*SVF* 2.458). Galen again says that "every plant is directed by *physis*, and every animal by *physis* and *psychē* together; if at any rate all we men use the name *physis* for the cause of feeding and growth and such activities, and use *psychē* for the cause of sensation and self-movement" (*SVF* 2.718). These texts are mutually consistent, and entitle us to conclude that the dominant Stoic doctrine distinguished the *pneuma* which changes from physis to soul from the *pneuma* responsible for bodily coherence and growth after an animal is born.

As Long himself indicates, his position in this matter differs considerably from that of Bonhöffer. In the sequence of *hexis, physis, psychē, logikē psychē*, the higher level, claims Bonhöffer, also contains the lower ones. (Cf. D.E. Hahm, *The Origins of Stoic Cosmology* [Columbus 1977]: "Each form of the *pneuma* includes all of the forms below it, but adds an additional psychic function;" D.L.7.148; Philo, LA 2.22.) The *hektikon* and *physikon pneuma* in animals and men is not a *pneuma* separate from the *psychikon*; instead the *psychikon pneuma* (in men the *logikon*) as such accomplishes whatever in inorganic things is done by the *hektikon* and in plants by the *physikon*. This is deduced from D.L.7.138, which implies that one and the same *pneuma* in men functions in the form of *hexis, physis,* and *logos*. (For Long this passage only implies the distinction between two senses of soul referred to by Sextus Empiricus, *Adv. Math.* 7.234: 1) "that which holds together the whole compound, 2) the *hēgemonikon*.) It is further confirmed by a statement of Nemesius (*SVF* 2.451) to the effect that the Stoics also attributed growth and the external formation and shaping of the body (*megethōn kai poiotētōn apotelestikēn einai*) to the power of soul (Bonhöffer 69, 105).

Long's interpretation appears to be similar to that of Ludwig Stein (*Die Erkenntnistheorie der Stoa* [Berlin 1888] 105-107), although the latter deals with this question only very briefly and does not marshal the important evidence from Galen and Philo. Stein begins by quoting Sextus 7.234, which he explains as follows. The *pneuma* of the world is present in every body in varying degrees of density or subtlety as its *synektikē dynamis*. The human body must therefore also contain this power of coherence, and this is the entire soul which pervades the body throughout (*krasis di' holōn*). But man possesses in addition a more subtle form of the cosmic pneuma, the *hēgemonikon*. Since both are similar in substance, the terms for them are readily exchanged. Thus, the corpse has lost its *hēgemonikon*, though it retains a degree of soul pneuma of the denser type. (For Bonhöffer, at death only *heksis* remains, whereas the *psychē* simply disappears; it does not separate itself from the body. The *hēgemonikon*, on the other hand, is separated from the body.)

Turning back to the Philonic evidence, I should like tentatively to offer an alternative explanation of its intent. Philo, it seems to me, is singling out those parts of the human body which the Stoics believed remained under the control of *hektikon* and *physikon pneuma* even after the *psychikon* (*logikon*) took control over all the rest. He particularly emphasizes the fact that the bones in us are similar to stones, and the nails and hair are similar to plants. It is thus implied that the other bodily constituents, such as flesh, skin, and blood, which are unlike stones or plants, are now under the control of the *hēgemonikon*. My position is therefore somewhere between that of Bonhöffer on the one hand, and Stein and Long on the other. The Stoics apparently believed that the higher levels of *pneuma* subsume those below them, so that in man, the *hēgemonikon*[1] is in control of all bodily conditions and functions, with the sole exception of the bones, which are governed by a *hektikon pneuma*, and the nails and hair which are governed by a *physikon pneuma*.

---

[1] Although the majority of the Stoics located the *hēgemonikon* in the heart, some Stoics, according to Philodemus (*De Pietate* 15), located it in the head (*SVF* 2.910; 3.33; Diog. Baby.).

[*Appended Note:* Shortly after the Colloquy, I found a Philonic passage which clearly confirms my interpretation of the evidence from *LA* 2.22. In *Spec.* 1.254, Philo writes: "The part, therefore, which his zeal prompted him to take was one which can be removed without causing either pain or mutilation. He cut off the hairs of his head like the superfluous branches of the part of the body which has 'growth' like a tree."]

MINUTES OF THE COLLOQUY OF 3 JUNE 1979

List of Participants

Professor at the *Institute for Advanced Study, Princeton; and the University of Liverpool*
Anthony A. Long *(Greek)*

Professors at the *University of California, Berkeley*
William S. Anderson *(Classics)*
Alan Code *(Philosophy)*
John Dillon *(Classics)*
Erich S. Gruen *(History)*
James L. Jarrett *(Philosophy of Education)*
Anitra Bingham Kolenkow *(Lecturer, Religious Studies)*
John W. Leopold *(Rhetoric)*
Charles E. Murgia *(Classics)*
Thomas G. Rosenmeyer *(Greek and Comparative Literature)*
Wayne Shumaker *(English, Emeritus)*
Tu Wei-ming *(History)*

Professors at the *Graduate Theological Union*
Marvin Brown *(Visiting Scholar)*
Michael J. Buckley *(Systematic Theology)*
Michael L. Cook *(Systematic Theology)*
Mary Ann Donovan *(Historical Theology)*
Loretta Dornisch *(Visiting Scholar)*
Victor R. Gold *(Old Testament)*
Edward C. Hobbs *(Theology and Hermeneutics)*
Thomas W. Leahy *(Biblical Studies)*
Ted F. Peters *(Systematic Theology)*
David Winston *(Hellenistic and Judaic Studies)*
John H. Wright *(Systematic Theology)*
Wilhelm Wuellner *(New Testament)*

Professors at *Other Colleges and Universities*
Otto E. Guttentag *(U. of California, S.F.: Medical Philosophy, Emeritus)*
Ludwig Koenen *(U. of Michigan, Ann Arbor: Papyrology)*
Irene Lawrence *(U. of California, Davis: Lecturer, Religious Studies)*
George S. Riggan *(Hartford Seminary Foundation: Systematic Theology, Emer.)*
James Royse *(San Francisco State: Philosophy)*
Fred Veltman *(Pacific Union College: New Testament)*

Students
David Elliott-Manrique *(GTU)*
John Engeln *(GTU)*
Arthur J. Lenti *(GTU)*
Daryl Schmidt *(GTU)*
Allan Silverman *(UCB)*
Lavette Teague *(GTU)*

MINUTES OF THE COLLOQUY OF 3 JUNE 1979

THE DISCUSSION

Summarized by Irene Lawrence

Long: As Professor Michael Frede says,* "Bodies and souls are a dangerous matter," so it is a good thing to band together to discuss them. We are fairly familiar with the notion of soul and body if it is related to some sort of dualist metaphysics (for example, Plato's). But what are we to make of the distinction when the soul itself is said to be a body of some kind? My respondents have rightly focussed on that.

On p. 3, I said provisionally that, for the Stoics, a human being "is a composite of a body, in the ordinary sense of body, and a *psyche* which is a body in some other sense." Frede suggests that this would most probably be taken to imply a contrast between body and soul, based on the (implicit) theory that "our body is opposed to our soul or our mind as our real self." This contrast (he argues) presupposes that the soul or self is not a physical part of what we regard as our physical body. But the Stoics, he maintains, do take "the soul itself to be a material constituent of the physical body which we tend to regard as our body."

I would reply that Frede is correct in detecting a contrast; but I do not agree with him about its inapplicability to the Stoics. They do not maintain that the soul *simpliciter* is a material constituent of the physical body which we regard as our body, the structure of flesh, blood, and bones; rather, they say that it is a material constituent of the *animal* or *human being* (p. 8, cf. p. 13). But Frede could reply, as he does in discussing p. 6 of my paper, that it is the soul which is responsible for structuring the body, and that it does so by its physical presence throughout the body. Therefore, perhaps he would say, the soul is a physical part of the body as we ordinarily understand our body.

This may be what the Stoics should have said, but I do not think it is what they did say or wanted to say. They inherited the distinction between soul and body, and they were Aristotelian enough to regard that distinction, in certain contexts, as one of form and matter. Form in Stoicism, however, is "matter in a certain state" (*hyle pos echousa*), and I do not think that they regarded "certain states" as "parts" of any body, but as the particular body itself, i.e., something identifiable by its structure and properties. This is why I argue on p. 6 that the notion of the (animal or human) body already requires the notion of soul, in order that it may be an organized structure of flesh, blood, and bones. It is of the body as that structure that the Stoics ordinarily speak when they say that the body is compounded with the soul to constitute the animal or human being. So in that expression, soul is ordinarily used by the Stoics in a specific sense, not to account for the animal's or human's flesh, blood, and bones, but to account for certain vital functions which living bodies have in addition to their flesh, blood, and bones.

_____

*In a critique which arrived too late for use in the Colloquy.

Frede, perhaps rightly, criticizes me for saying that the notion of the soul as holding the body together rules out any clear distinction between body and soul. He stresses the fact that, in the general analysis of all "unified" bodies, a clear distinction between the items of the "complete blending" is required. But, as he also points out, "the body minus the *pneuma* which makes it the kind of animal and the particular animal it is," is not an informative answer to the question of what the body is apart from the soul. The body in this sense would presumably be something like my rejected answer on p. 6. Frede helpfully distinguishes between bodies as objects (e.g., stones) and bodies as bits of stuff (quite abstract and theoretical) which are constituents of the complete blending which gives rise to bodies as objects.

It might be useful to reformulate my distinction between two senses of soul along these lines:

1. An animal is a composite of body and soul, held together by the soul. (Here body and soul are used in highly abstract ways, corresponding to the basic Stoic principles, *hyle* and *logos*, neither of which constitutes an object in any straightforward sense.)

2. An animal is a composite of body and soul. (Here body and soul are used in highly specific ways, such that each does refer to an object, viz. a body, an organized structure of flesh, blood, and bones; and a soul which is the sentient and kinetic entity present in the structure and presumed, in humans, to be capable to existing in separation from that structure.)

All the respondents have rightly pressed further on the question of how far the soul is to be taken in these two ways, and what their relationship is. Professor Winston suggests that my "vegetative" function of a human being or animal, which goes along with the body in my account, is perhaps to be restricted to hair and nails. That may have been what Philo wanted to say, but not the Stoics in general. The passage quoted from Nemesius (p. 22) does not seem to me to be about the soul at all; its subject is *pneuma*, divine breath-- and not all *pneuma* is soul.

For our main issue for discussion, we should focus as sharply as we can on the distinction between soul and body for the Stoics, and on whether we do need to distinguish two kinds of souls, or functions of souls, or soul doing different jobs in different contexts.

Wuellner: You have restricted yourself to early and main Stoicism.

Long: There is, of course, the problem that the evidence for early Stoicism is so fragmentary. So I have talked about "the (early) Stoics" without distinguishing between individuals. There do not seem to be any fundamental differences among them, although this is conjectural.

Gruen: I miss a sense of historical development. On p. 2, you admit a contrast between the early and the late Stoics. Were there other aspects of the idea of soul and body that might have developed and changed? Might some of the Stoic ideas be reactions or responses to criticisms made by Platonists or Peripatetics?

Long: I deliberately took an analytical approach, because the historical approach is limited. The evidence I used would be generally taken to apply to Chrysippus. It is clear that there was an important shift with Posidonius, who treated the soul in a more Platonic way, as something which, by its very nature, admitted of both rational and irrational faculties. But this is a topic in itself. If there is a historical framework here, it is the theories of Plato and Aristotle. The Stoic theory was not prompted by criticisms; if anything, it might *be* criticism, particularly of Aristotelian attitudes.

Rosenmeyer: It is possible to think of *soma* in terms of density or in terms of structure. Could soul be body with density only, and no structure?

Long: Clearly, the minimum for any body is three-dimensionality and mass, or density. The "body"--flesh, blood, bones--is primarily constituted by the denser, inert, elements, while the soul is constituted by the finer, active, elements. But we cannot make the human soul *too* fluid, because it is supposed to survive the death of the body.

Rosenmeyer: I was not trying to distinguish between elements, but to suggest that soul-matter might lend itself to a *soma* without structure, whereas to the usual "body" structure is very important.

Long: The Stoics use various spatial images to help picture the soul. For example, the spider represents the *hegemonikon*, and the strands of its web correspond to the sensory *pneumata*, etc. And they use the image of the octopus. The soul is pictured as extending spatially through the body.

Rosenmeyer: The very fact that they have to use images suggests that something is missing. And if the soul has structure only in relation to the body, then it may have no structure as soul.

Shumaker: I was surprised that there is no *tertium quid* between the soul as *soma* and the soul as *psyche*. In Renaissance thought, differences of this sort were always brought together by means of something intermediate. But perhaps communication would here be made possible because of the elements: fire shares with air heat, and air shares with water moisture, and so on. In the Renaissance there were three souls, not seven: the vegetative, the sensitive, and the rational.

Long: On the one hand, there is a sharp disjunction between the body and the soul, which looks rather Platonic, and which comes up in the Stoics' ethical theory. On the other hand, the body itself has a form, and its form is due to the activity of the active principle in the universe, the *pneuma*. *Pneuma* at a higher degree of tension will produce soul in the strict sense. So they had a continuum view: everything in the universe can be explained in terms of the different qualifications *pneuma* introduces into matter, that which has the potentiality to take on properties.

Shumaker: *Pneuma* may be exactly what I was looking for.

Long: A number of Church Fathers, influenced by the Stoics and by St. Paul (1 Th 5:23)--for instance, Tatian (see Spanneut, *Le stoïcisme des pères de l'église*[2], 138-140)--talk of *soma*, *psyche*, and *pneuma* to explain human beings, and the *pneuma* is something like the divine spirit.

Koenen: This question may be connected with speculation outside the Stoic school, according to which the body is actually the body of the soul, and the soul is the body of the *nous*. Such ideas were particularly popular in Middle

Platonism and the Church Fathers of Alexandria. They assumed not just the Platonic dualism of soul and body, but a series of two different bodies, the second less dense than the first. According to Porphyrios, the soul is not dressed at once with the muddy body, but on her descent through the planets the soul is clad with more and more wrappings preparing it for the final garment of the earthen body. The Stoic distinction between the "spiritual" and dense body belongs to the same tradition which developed from the interpretation of Plato.*

Murgia: There seems to be a problem in logic here. The paper's title is "Soul and Body in Stoicism." But "body" has several different meanings. The soul is body by definition, in the sense that it belongs to one of the four elements. Now, the human body has at least two senses, possibly three. One sense is the living body; another sense is the corpse. We cannot assume that the two are the same. And the third sense in this context is "that which the soul leaves." It remains to be seen whether that is the same as the corpse, or the living body, or something else. We need to use "body" carefully. On the middle of p. 6, for example, you say, "For these Stoics, Sextus continues, it is only the soul in the latter sense which is invoked *when we say that man is composed of body and soul*, or that death is the separation of soul from body. . . . Soul in the sense, 'that which holds together the whole compound,' rules out any clear distinction between soul and body. Even a corpse, and all the more so a skeleton, possesses coherence over time." In terms of logic, the *hexis* of a corpse is not the same as the *hexis* of a living body. So there is no logical problem in having soul as *hexis* leave the living body, and having a *hexis* of the corpse remain. The Stoics were not logically compelled to have two senses of the word "soul."

Silverman: Also on p. 6, you say that *"hexis* and *nous* are both functions of *pneuma* at different degrees of tension." What is the origin or cause of the different degrees of tension, and what is the connection between change in tension and rationality?

Long: The Stoics try to explain all phenomena in terms of the different quali-

---

*Porphyrios, *In Macrobius* 1.1.11 (p. 47, 15ff; Numenius, *Test.* 47 p. 107 Leeman). The soul is *to pneumatikon ochema* or *to lepton* (*leptomeres* [see also *SVF* II 780]; *augoeides; aitherodes*) *soma*, the body is called *geinon* (*pachu; pachuteron; geodes*) *soma*; cf. E. R. Dodds, Proclus, *The Elements of Theology* (Oxford 1933) 313ff.; M. A. Elferink, *La descente de l'âme d'apres Macrobe* (Leiden 1968) nn. 95. 98. and 109; B. J. Stricker, "augoeides soma," *Outheidk. Mededel. uit het Rijksmus. te Leiden* 43 (1963) 4ff.; F. W. Cremer, *Die chaldäischen Orakel und Jamblich, De mysteriis* (Meisenheim 1969) 137; O. Geudtner, *Die Seelenlehre der chaldäischen Orakel* (Meisenheim 1971) 18ff.; J. Dillon, *The Middle Platonists* (Ithaca 1977) 175f. [on Philon's *psyche psyches*] and 375ff.; A. Henrichs & L. Koenen, *ZPE* 19 (1975) 73f. For Origen see, e.g., *De princ.* 1.4.1. GCS 5, 64, 12f. (p. 204f. H. Görgemanns & H. Karpp); 2.2.2 GCS 112, 24 (p. 298 Görgem. & Karpp) and frequently; Didymos, *In Gen.* 107, 4ff. (P. Nautin & L. Doutreleau, Did. l'Aveugle, Sur la Genèse I Paris 1976 248ff.); U. u. D. Hagedorn & L. Koenen, *Didymos der Blinde,* Kommentar zu Hiob III (Bonn 1968) 257ff. n. 101; L. Koenen, "From Baptism to the Gnosis of Manichaeism," *Proceedings of the Intern. Conference on Gnosticism at Yale* (in print at Brill), n. 83. - The so-called Pauline *Pneuma* is a different story; cf. A. Henrichs & L. Koenen, *ZPE* 5 (1970) 186ff.

fications that the active principle introduces into the potential or passive principle. The active principle is a self-moving body. By the principle of economy, they account for all phenomena in terms of the changes in the interaction of these two principles. "Tension" seems an appropriate property for *pneuma*.

One answer about origin that the Stoics give is that the body in gestation develops before the soul; a structure of flesh, blood, and bones must come into being before psychic functions. (They could have said with Aristotle that the soul starts like a plant, but becomes an animal in the course of gestation. But they did not.) They wanted a multiplicity, if not of souls, at least of effects generated by the soul, because there are properties shared by humans with stones, others with plants, others with animals, others which mark humans off. If one soul does all that, it must have different functions or even parts. The Stoics were trying to present the evolution of life in the individual as a developing sequence. The question which Professor Kerferd raised remains: are we to speak of two kinds of souls, or of one soul with different functions? As he points out, the functions are sometimes simultaneous.

Jarrett: From an Aristotelian point of view, regarding the material part of soul as potentiality and the form as actuality, is there anything approximating the second entelechy? Is there the notion of soul as having *telos*, as representing in some sense that which the body is achieving or aspiring to?

Long: Certainly, if you mean the living body. Undoubtedly, the soul is what the body in that sense is for. It is the goal of human beings to live a rational life, which is to cultivate the soul.

Dillon: Professor Murgia suggested that the *hexis* of a rational, living body can be seen as a different entity, or as having a different degree of coherence from that of, say, a skeleton. The soul's arising seems problematical now. I note an admittedly dismal doxographical definition of the rising of the soul from a scholion on the *Iliad*: "The soul is *pneuma* arising in the body and an exhalation involving sense perception given off from the moist parts of the body" (*SVF* 2.778). That makes the soul very secondary, a kind of brandy given off by the body.

At a certain stage of complexity--even irrational, certainly rational--this kind of *pneuma* becomes a separate body. One objection to Professor Long is actually an objection against the Stoics: why not *hexis* and *physis* as separate bodies? All the manifestations of the *pneuma* which form any entities seem to be exhalations or degrees of tension arising in the body, but the Stoics--for quasi-political reasons, or because they had inherited the notion of soul and could not get rid of it--at a certain stage thought that there were *two* bodies involved, in total mixture.

Hexis is associated with stone, wood, and other objects; it holds them together. Souls of rational people survive, held together only by some sort of *hexis*, which is not usually associated with souls. And some souls hold together better than others; those of wise men hold together the best. These are complaints addressed to Chrysippus, not to Professor Long.

Long: The soul cannot arise until the moment of birth, because the animal has to breath in the *pneuma* from the external environment.

Wuellner: So the Stoics would not have opposed abortion.

Long: The soul seems to need two kinds of food: the blood (another reason the body has to be formed first), and the external air.

Hobbs: Professor Long raised the question of the Church Fathers who appealed to St. Paul for a tripartite distinction among *soma, psyche,* and *pneuma.* They were really appealing to the Pauline school, especially to the Pastor, much later than Paul. For Paul, *psyche* was a very unimportant term, meaning not much more than the self as living. His concern was *soma,* and he distinguished between *soma sarkikon* and *soma pneumatikon.* And *soma* is never used by Paul about a corpse, so it does not mean "body" in the detective's sense: "Where's the body?" The *soma* for Paul is the living self, and the term he often brings into connection with it is not *psyche,* as the Stoics, but *nous.* Paul is working out of a framework as much informed by his Biblical background and his Hebrew traditions as by popular philosophy.

Gold: First, it is sometimes suggested that the book of Qoheleth or Ecclesiastes has some Stoic material in it. Second, if this be true, as closely related as body and soul are in this thought, why did the notion of a composite resurrection of body and soul never occur?

Long: First, I do not know about Qoheleth. Second, one of the reasons why some of the apologists--Tertullian and Irenaeus, for example--use a Stoic rather than a Platonic model for the human being is precisely because of the problem of the resurrection. They think that Platonic dualism disposes of the body. But for a pagan philosopher, there is no problem about *how* we can have resurrection, but *why* we should have it at all. Because the Stoics think that the soul of a human is *pneuma* at a degree of tension that corresponds more or less to that of the universal divine *pneuma,* when it leaves the body there is no reason for it to perish. That does not explain the problem of individual survival. The problem of the body ought to have worried Plato, given his notion of the soul's migration, but not the Stoics.

Donovan: There are several sets of texts, particularly at the end of the second and in the early third centuries that illustrate very well what was made of this kind of thinking by some Church Fathers. Irenaeus has anthropology functioning in the service of a theology, showing what a human being must be composed of because of what he or she is destined for. When he deals with the resurrection, he understands the human person to be flesh, spirit, and spirit of God (cf. Adv. Haer. V, 6,1 and V, 9,1). The human person must be intimately conjoined with the spirit which is the divine spirit, in order to reach the goal of our full humanity, what was soon afterward called deification.

A near contemporary is Tertullian, and there I have more questions than answers. The questions come not so much out of his anthropology as out of his Trinitarian theology. For example, he talks of God as body (Adv. Prax. VII, 8), spirit as body (Adv. Prax. VIII, 4), and soul as body (Adv. Marc. V, 15, 8), but he is clearly not being crassly materialistic.

Dillon: I am not clear how anyone who believed in the resurrection of the body could take much consolation from any Greek philosophy--unless they believed in the resurrection of a pneumatic body.

Long: Tertullian uses the concept of a "total mélange," although not entirely in a Stoic way, because he seems to suppose that it is always in some way the state of the person. Even the resurrected self is that kind of composite.

Donovan: Often in people like Tertullian and Irenaeus, and even more strongly in Clement of Alexandria, the vocabulary needs to be rethought in accordance with their theological presuppositions. Understanding a term as used in philosophy is not enough to understand a Father's intention. There is always some transformation.

Long: The Stoics must have realized that although a corpse has some kind of *hexis*, it is not the sort of *hexis* that will last very long.

Murgia: It particularly lacks the capacity for regeneration.

Long: I claimed that the notion of soul as "that which holds the body together" ruled out a clear distinction between soul and body. If this is not so, then what is the body, what is that identifiable entity that the soul holds together? Is it not just the body with form already?

Murgia: But the term "body" keeps changing its sense. Your alternatives 2 and 3 on p. 6 could both be right of the same Stoic, but with "body" being used in a different sense. Vergil [in *Aen.* 6(724-751), which is influenced by Stoicism], who was a pseudo-Stoic, took the body to be just earth: the corpse is the equivalent of *terra*, and the soul when it leaves the body must be purged with earth, air, and water in the underworld.

Long: But if living bodies are composites of a soul and a body, then one cannot regard the living body as just earth and water occupying a point in space.

Murgia: But when one says that the soul leaves the living body, what is left is not the living body. The element of "living" leaves with the soul. The living body is a mixture of soul and body, but when separated, the soul may leave earth and water behind. The "living body" is a composite; when the soul leaves it, the remaining "body" is a different concept.

Winston: Regarding resurrection, what appealed to the Christians about the Stoics was that after the *ekpyrosis* everything would be reconstituted exactly as it was before. Socrates will live again.*

    One of the Stoics' proofs of the corporeality of the soul, which Professor Long mentions on p. 8 and in n. 18, is that children resemble their parents not only in physical characteristics but in mental ones also. But only bodies can resemble each other; therefore, the soul must be corporeal. Professor Long asks why *lekta* or propositions could not resemble each other. Perhaps, since for the Stoics all bodies must differ from each other, they must be either different or resemble each other. But *lekta* either differ from each other or are identical. If they seem to resemble each other, they are really identical *lekta*.

Teague: What phenomena would one appeal to as evidence in discussing the survival

---

    *See H. Wolfson, *Religious Philosophy* (Cambridge, 1961): 74-75: "An analogy between these two beliefs [the Stoic doctrine of palingenesis and the Christian doctrine of resurrection] is sometimes suggested by the Fathers themselves. Thus Tatian (*Orat. ad Graec.* 6) and Clement of Alexandria (*Strom.* 5.1.9) and Origen (*Contr. Cels.* 5.20) hint at such an analogy, and Lactantius (*Div. Inst.* 7.23) and Augustine (*Civ. Dei* 22.28) explicitly advance it as a proof for the possibility of resurrection, and Nemesius quotes it as something said by "some people." (*Nat. Hom.* 38)

of the soul? If the soul is what holds the body together, evidence might be that it takes a while for a body to decompose, and that hair, beard, and nails continue to grow after death. To what evidence does one appeal for the survival of the soul of a wise man? Perhaps to his continuing influence?

Long: The difficulty Professor Murgia has raised applies again. Although something survives, the corpse is clearly not the living body. The soul is no longer an activating soul.

Murgia: An Epicurean argument talks of a cut-off hand still wriggling by the side of the chariot. Epicurus did not believe in immortality, but he did believe that parts of the principle of life are so intermingled that they do not all get out at once.

Dillon: Do higher level souls subsume the lower ones, or do they just sit on top of them? The Stoics seem to be in a bind about how much soul leaves. (Also the Platonists and the Christians!) If the soul is immortal or survives, then it carries all eight parts with it. But what does it do with these now useless parts? Yet to hold together until the *ekpyrosis* it needs a fair measure of *hexis*. And the body has its *hexis*, so now there are two *hexeis*. They really should not have gotten into this.

Winston: My impression is that only the *hegemonikon* can be separated and survive the body as the subtlest type of *pneuma*, supposedly rejoining the *aether*. It joins as a separate focus of *pneuma*. The *psyche*, the animal soul, is simply dispersed; it is not strong or subtle enough to retain its own identity after death. The only thing left is *hexis*, because everything has *hexis*.

Murgia: So the soul also must have *hexis*, even when separated from the body?

Winston: I assume that the higher levels subsume the lower, so the highest kind of soul certainly has *hexis*.

Long: Its *hexis* is its *logos*. It is true for the Stoic that a stone consists of two bodies. It is a unified body; and its *hexis* is a body distinct from the earth and water which it is holding together. But that *hexis*, of course, does not survive the stone's being hit with a sledgehammer, since its only job was to hold the earth and water together. But the job of *logike psyche* is not to hold the bones together; the *pneuma* of the body does that. So it does have an identity of its own.

Dillon: It seems, if we go back to first principles, that there is the active principle, *pneuma*, and the passive principle. The whole universe is held together by a cosmic *hexis*, the interpenetration of the active principle and the passive. But each separate body consists of active and passive principles, and therefore the soul has a body--a very pure, pneumatic, fiery one--even when it is by itself.

Long: It has two bodies, because it is a composite of fire and air.

Dillon: Does it have both active and passive principles?

Winston: There is always passive principle in the universe, so even if it is out of one particular body, it is in another.

Wright: The section of the plurality of souls or principles contains the same sort of debate that went on in the Middle Ages. One of the problems that Thomas Aquinas ran into, and for which he was condemned by the University of Paris, was that he maintained the unicity of the human soul, that only one soul was the principle of all functions. One and the same principle which makes a person a body makes him human. Since the problem arises for the Stoic, and in the Middle Ages, does it not arise for us, too? We also need to think about what it is that makes us human.

Kolenkow: Professor Dillon quoted a description of the soul going out of the moist parts of the body. Origen says that prophecy enters the body through the pores. Isn't this rather a more general philosophical medical view than merely Stoic?

Dillon: Origen had a different view of body after the resurrection, more of a pneumatic body. It is not unlike the middle Platonic notion of the vehicle of the rational soul. It would have been influenced by Stoic theorizing, and was an acceptable way of explaining how a soul could survive as a separate entity. The Stoics did not address themselves to that, nor did the Platonists; Plotinus agonized over it.

Murgia: When a stone, which has *hexis*, is struck with a hammer, the *hexis* does not continue. Does it split into smaller *hexeis* for the smaller parts, or is it destroyed, and *hexeis* for the pebbles generated? For an Aristotelian, for instance, the forms of the whole would be destroyed and new forms generated.

Winston: The amount of body in the Stoic universe is stable; it cannot change. The component parts retain small *pneumata* of *hexis*.

Murgia: Then if they were consistent about the soul vs. the body, a basic amount of *hexis* would go off with the soul, and some would remain as the *hexis* of the corpse.

Long: But there were different kinds of *hexeis*. The *hexis* which is the rational soul is a different kind from that which accounts for the bones.

Murgia: But if the soul in the living body subsumes all of those, then the parts which concern the soul go off with the soul, and those which concern the body stay with it. The living body will have elements which are part of the soul.

Winston: The Stoics could have seen that a skeleton generally remains indefinitely, so they assumed that it retained *hexis*. But the higher principle of the body's unity took over the function of *hexis*. Hence when the *psyche* disperses, that part decays very quickly. The *hegemonikon* which left is all that survives as a separately identifiable type of *pneuma*.

Murgia: Part of the *hexis* is subsumed under the *hegemonikon* and stays, and part is dispersed, and part stays with the skeleton.

Winston: In the living body, the *hegemonikon* takes over all of the other functions except for the *hexis* of the bones and the *physis* of the hair and nails. Upon death, the *hegemonikon* leaves, and the *psyche* can no longer function for the blood, flesh, and skin, so all that is left is the *hexis* of the bones, and the *physis* of the hair and nails.

Long: That is a coherent picture, but if the *hegemonikon* is responsible for the *hexis* of all parts of the body while it is alive, except for the bones, hair, and nails, then what about the embryological theory which says that all the organs, particularly the heart, have to come first?

Winston: While an embryo, it is all on the level of a *physis*; it is a plant. There is no *psyche* or *hegemonikon*.

Long: But given that things are holding together in this plant-like entity, why does the newly-existing *psyche* have to be responsible for that?

Winston: Because as soon as the higher enters, it takes over the functions of the lower.

Long: If the *psyche* as *hegemonikon* is responsible for all the bodily functions aside from the exceptions, why is that not singled out in the specific functions of the *hegemonikon*?

Winston: The most characteristic and distinctive quality of the *hegemonikon* is its rational function, so that is emphasized. The rest is taken for granted.

Long: That seems unlikely. At least, it is a very strange gap. The vegetative is a very important part of the living organism, according to this story. The body as formed can perform this function without direction from the *hegemonikon*; we do not have to think about making our heart beat. The function of the human *hegemonikon* is to perform rational acts.

Winston: Probably the *hegemonikon* is so subtle that it interpenetrates and can influence everything. Of course, we do not really know. This is pure speculation.

Wright: That is Thomas's position.

Koenen: The Stoicism of Christian authors such as Origen is not so much real Stoicism as a kind of philosophical *koine*.

Dillon: Origen is more a Platonist.

Koenen: In Origen, a lot of Stoic terminology is used, including *hegemonikon*, but it is very uncertain how much real Stoic thought is present.

Leopold: There is a very curious statement of Cicero, who denies that *cohaerentia* applies to fragments of stone or wood, but says it does apply to trees and animals and humans, and to the universe as a whole. Is this just Cicero's mistake, or is it an unorthodox version of the *hexis/physis* theory?

Long: When a tree dies, we have the corpse problem again. We had a unified body; now we have a dead unified body. A fragment of wood is not a unified body in the sense that it could fall under any kind of species; it is not an organism. It is probably the same with bits of stone. In the Stoic universe, anything that has extension in space *must* have some kind of *hexis*, because the active and passive principles never exist apart. There is always *pneuma* acting on matter, and its most basic action is holding, or *hexis*. Whether Cicero made a mistake would depend on the context.

Leopold: The context was *cohaerentia* and the items in the universe as a whole.

Long: To say "bits of stone" implies the notion of a whole of which the bits were once part. To explain why that whole no longer exists, the Stoics inferred a *hexis* that had ceased to exist. Then the question can be asked again of each individual fragment, since matter is infinitely divisible. Presumably they are operating by a rule of thumb notion about what constitutes a stone as distinct from a bit of stone.

Jarrett: I was struck by the extent to which "soul" is conceived of in terms of an organizational, unifying principle with respect to matter, and with how little attention was paid to soul as subject, as "I," as agent. That may be a post-Cartesian point of view. But the relation in Stoicism between the soul and divinity, and providence, and creative daemon, would seem to allow for that emphasis too.

Long: I touched on that at the end of the paper, but that particular aspect was not what I was trying to develop here. There is a great deal of material which does focus on the "I," ethical theory in particular. It is not quite Cartesian; it does not start from consciousness.

Jarrett: I would have supposed that from that other point of view the body could be seen as an instrumentality of this agency, leading to a different focus on the relationship.

Long: I suggest that on the last page. But it seemed worth looking at "body" here, since it may be a real problem for the Stoics.

Hobbs: To footnote Professor Koenen's caveat and Professor Donovan's point: the first Christian theologian, St. Paul, uses Stoic formulations--blessings and benedictions, lists of virtues and vices, and so on--but he is just borrowing them out of the air, as conventions or popular philosophy. Despite his use of phraseology and even whole sentences, he is not a Stoic, and his material cannot be interpreted in terms of Stoicism. It is dangerous to imagine that any Church Father's Stoic terminology operates in any sense that would be acceptable to a Stoic philosopher.

Wright: Another footnote: a classic Stoic description of God was *pronoia*, *providentia*. This is superimposed on the Christian view which comes out of the Bible and distorts it. It produced intellectual indigestion in Christian theology for centuries.

Shumaker: Does "tension" vary inversely with "density"? It seems that if tension means something like tightness, it would be found in a stone more than in a soul.

Long: *Pneuma* physics is presumably a very difficult subject. On the one hand, the soul has an extremely fine, tenuous, quality, such that it is analogous to the heat which penetrates a piece of metal. On the other hand, the soul has a tension such that it can survive independently of the body.

Teague: Taking a physical analogy, the finer the wire that is pulled with the same force, the greater the stress.

Wright: There are a number of remarkable analogies between the thought of the Stoics and that of Teilhard de Chardin. Chardin's "within" and "without" correspond roughly to the soul and the body. It is under the personalizing presence of God that matter complexifies. Greater complexity in the without corresponds to greater intensity in the within.

Dillon: As Professor Wright remarked earlier, this is not a dead issue, unless one tries to abolish the mind altogether, whether by naive or by sophisticated reductionism. The fact that the Stoics clung to the notion of soul, inherited from Aristotle, caused them trouble. The soul cannot enter just any body; it must be the exhalation of a body that potentially has rational life. (Platonism, though, seems to think differently.) But for the Stoic, the degree of tension of *pneuma* is conditioned by the type of body.

Long: It is not a case of a soul getting into a body, but of a body developing so that at birth breath is sufficient to activate whatever was growing as the soul. Some of these notions might have developed to try to solve some of the problems Aristotle gets into. Aristotle thinks that there is a *symphyton pneuma*, or connate breath, to mediate between the body and the soul (where the soul is thought of as efficient cause). There, *pneuma* is a kind of halfway house, having something in common with both the body and the soul. It will depend on one's assessment of Aristotle's causal theory whether one thinks that his soul as form or actuality will really answer questions about what makes bodies move. The Stoics supposed that only bodies can move bodies. So the *symphyton pneuma* is promoted to the full soul. They still need "soul" to distinguish between bodies as things extending in space and life functions, behavior patterns, potentialities.

Koenen: The notion of the soul creating its own body is the opposite of Origen's notion, where the soul gets the body it deserves.

Dillon: For Origen, Stoic terminology had become assimilated to a Platonic model. A lot of middle Platonists would be grossly offended if they were called Stoics, or even accused of using Stoic terminology. Their idea is of immaterial souls descending in various degrees into bodies, not bodies producing souls. They used the notion of pneumatic body or body of fire to bridge an awkward conjunction.

Silverman: It appears that the rational soul or *hegemonikon* either has sufficient tension to be rational when it enters the body, or the human body somehow bequeaths the rationality to the soul. If the latter, then the soul should become irrational when it departs from the body.

Long: Souls do not "enter" bodies. The Stoics talked of something which governs the potential living thing, the embryo, turning into something else. It is a change, not an entrance; the already existing *physis* changes into soul, activated by the external breath. It is unfortunate that the Stoics used the term "parts" of the soul. But there is no question that only the *hegemonikon* survives, because the subordinate parts are quite specifically related to bodily regions. The *hegemonikon* can certainly survive, even without *phone*. Someone may need to vocalize to learn not only to speak but to think. But once he has learned to think, he need no longer vocalize. The surviving *hegemonikon* presumably keeps all its learned dispositions. And since it is rational through and through, then it must survive as a purely rational entity.

Lenti: What is the origin of the soul for the Stoics? And is what survives identical to the original entity, or is it different?

Long: What survives is very different from what begins, because a life has been lived, and all kinds of dispositions and learnings are carried with the surviving *hegemonikon*, determining its moral status and the length of its survival. We have only snippets of evidence about how the soul originates, but they are consistent. The fetus is a plant-like entity; the baby's first breath is sufficient to turn--

metaballein--the determining principle of that previous embryo into that of a potentially rational animal.

Wuellner: Is there any difference for the Stoic whether the soul lives in a male or a female body?

Long: I do not know of any difference.

Hobbs: They are better than Aristotle in that respect.

Long: They do say that semen must contain *pneuma* of a certain kind, *pneuma* which is potentially soul (*SVF* 1.128).

Shumaker: The fact that the organism must draw breath before being endowed with *pneuma* accounts for the fact that the ancient astrologers took the moment of birth rather than of conception as crucial for the horoscope.

Winston: Because the fetus was only a plant they could allow abortion.

Code: Could you clarify Frede's objection to your "body in the ordinary sense"?

Long: He asks in *what* ordinary sense. He suggests that the most obvious "ordinary sense" is the contrast that can be made if one has a theory that man consists of a soul or self which is non-physical, as distinguished from the physical body. He then argues that that cannot be a proper way of talking about the Stoics, because they do not have the notion of a non-physical soul or self. For them, the soul is a part of the physical body "in the ordinary sense."

Code: Does "non-physical" mean "non-material"?

Long: We do not have Frede here to ask.

Code: I would have thought that the four Aristotelian elements would determine what is physical.

Long: Frede is not talking about Greek philosophy here. He says: "This lack of clarity [meaning the lack of clarity in the distinction between body and soul] is somewhat obscured by the fact that it seems so obvious what the term 'body in this ordinary sense' refers to, namely to the physical body, which is our body. But if that seems so obvious to us, it is only because we presuppose that the self, the mind, or the soul, whatever they may be, are not themselves physical parts of the physical body which we regard as our body. The Stoics did not share this presupposition." So his point is that the Stoics *did* think of their soul as a part of what we here and now ordinarily regard as the physical body. I am doubtful. We do not ordinarily regard the capacity to think as part of the physical body. We would say the brain is part of the physical body, but only certain kinds of materialists would reduce the capacity to think to part of the body.

Code: But nor do we ordinarily mean by body "informed earth and water." It is not clear why a distinction between body and soul has to be made in terms of a distinction between body in the ordinary sense and some other kind of body, rather than in terms of one body, which is everything in this particular place, and within which one can make certain distinctions, none of which are "body in the ordinary sense."

Long: I agree, and I see the force of Frede's objections. But I think it is an objection to the Stoics rather than to the formulation. They think that there is a living organism occupying a finite space, and within that space is what they want to call the body, and also what they want to call the soul. One cannot divide the organism in such a way as to get just body or just soul. Then what I ask is what *is* the force of the Stoic distinction between body and soul; they clearly think there is some force to it. In Aristotelian terms, it is a distinction between form and matter. But for the Stoics, form is in some sense material. That is where the difficulty arises. It is a difficult subject, and I am grateful for everyone's comments.

SELECT BIBLIOGRAPHY OF A.A. LONG

"Sophocles' *Trachiniae* 539-40," *Classical Review* N.S. 13 (1963) 128-9.

"The Principles of Parmenides' Cosmogony," *Phronesis* 8 (1963) 90-107, reprinted in D. J. Furley and R. E. Allen edd. *Studies in Presocratic Philosophy* vol. 2 (London, 1975) 82-101.

"Sophocles' *Electra* 1251-2," *Classical Review* N.S. 14 (1964) 130-2.

"Abstract Terminology in Sophocles: some uses of -sis nouns," *AUMLA* 21 (1964) 53-64.

"Sophocles' *Ajax* 68-70, a reply to Professor Fraenkel," *Museum Helveticum* 21 (1964) 228-31.

"Thinking and Sense-perception in Empedocles; mysticism or materialism?", *Classical Quarterly* N.S. 16 (1966) 256-76.

"Carneades and the Stoic Telos," *Phronesis* 12 (1967) 59-90.

"Poisonous Growths in *Trachiniae*." *Greek, Roman and Byzantine Studies* 8 (1967) 275-8.

Language and Thought in Sophocles. A Study of Abstract Nouns and Poetic Technique (Athlone Press, London, 1968).

"Aristotle, *De anima* 424b31-425a5," *Hermes* 96 (1968) 372-4.

"Aristotle's Legacy to Stoic Ethics," *Bulletin of the Institute of Classical Studies* 15 (1968) 72-85.

"The Stoic Concept of Evil," *Philosophical Quarterly* 18 (1968) 329-43.

"Morals and Values in Homer," *Journal of Hellenic Studies* 90 (1970) 121-39.

"Stoic Determinism and Alexander of Aphrodisias *De Fato* i-xiv," *Archiv für Geschichte der Philosophie* 52 (1970) 246-66.

Problems in Stoicism. Edited, with Introduction. (Athlone Press, London, 1971).

"Language and Thought in Stoicism," *Problems in Stoicism,* 75-113.

"Freedom and Determinism in the Stoic Theory of Human Action," *Problems in Stoicism* 173-199.

"The Logical Basis of Stoic Ethics," *Proceedings of the Aristotelian Society* (1970-71) 85-104.

"Aisthesis, Prolepsis and Linguistic Theory in Epicurus," *Bulletin of the Institute of Classical Studies* 18 (1971) 114-33.

40

"Psychological Ideas in Antiquity," *Dictionary of the History of Ideas* ed. Philip Wiener (Scribner's New York, 1973) vol. 4, 1-9.

"Ethics of Stoicism," ibid. 319-22.

Hellenistic Philosophy, Stoics, Sceptics, Epicureans. (Duckworth, London, 1974). Spanish transl. *La Filosofía Helenística* (Biblioteca de la Revista de Occidente, Madrid, 1977).

"Empedocles' Cosmic Cycle in the 'Sixties'", *The Presocratics* ed. A.P.D. Mourelatos (Anchor Press, New York, 1974) 397-425.

"Alexander of Aphrodisias, *De fato* 190.26ff.," *Classical Quarterly* N.S. 25 (1975) 158-9.

"Heraclitus and Stoicism," *Philosophia* 5/6 (1975/6) 134-56.

"The Early Stoic Concept of Moral Choice," *Images of Man in Ancient and Medieval Thought.* Studia Gerardo Verbeke Dicata (Louvain, 1976) 79-92.

"Chance and Natural Law in Epicureanism," *Phronesis* 22 (1977) 63-88.

"Sophocles, *O.T.* 879-81," *Liverpool Classical Monthly* 3 (1978) 49-53.

"Dialectic and the Stoic Sage," *The Stoics* ed. John M. Rist (Berkeley and Los Angeles, 1978) 101-24.

"The Stoic distrinction between Truth and the True," *Les Stoiciens et leur logique* ed. J. Brunschwig (Vrins, Paris, 1978) 297-315.

"Timon of Phlius: Pyrrhonist and Satirist," *Proceedings of the Cambridge Philological Society* 204 (1978) 68-90.

"Sextus Empiricus on the Criterion of Truth," *Bulletin of the Institute of Classical Studies* 25 (1978) 35-49.

"Aristotle and the History of Greek Scepticism," *Aristotle* in series *Studies in Philosophy and the History of Philosophy* ed. Dominic O'Meara (Catholic University of America Press, Washington, D.C.: forthcoming).

"Stoicism: origins and growth of a Tradition," *Proceedings of the 75th Anniversary Meeting of the Classical Association:* forthcoming.

"Early Greek Philosophy" and "Aristotle and later Ancient Philosophy," *Cambridge History of Classical Literature* edd. P.E. Easterling and B.M.W. Knox: forthcoming.